Dear Friend:

Thank you for writing to us during our annual LETTER WEEK. It's always a special joy and encouragement to hear from our friends!

It's my special pleasure to be able to send you this copy of JESUS' PATTERN OF PRAYER by Dr. John MacArthur, Jr.

We trust this book will be a real help to you in your prayer life and also serve to remind you of our dependence on your serving with us through your prayers and support.

Thank you again for your faithful expressions of interest in these ministries of our Lord.

Sincerely in Christ,

E. Brandt Gustavson
Vice-President

EBG:lwp

Jesus' Pattern of Prayer

by
John MacArthur, Jr.

MOODY PRESS
CHICAGO

To all those faithful people whose prayers have touched the throne of God on behalf of my ministry, especially that faithful little flock who have met on Monday mornings for the last ten years

Contents

Preface

Because communion with God is so vital, the enemy seems constantly to introduce errors into the church's understanding of prayer. Every generation at every time faces the necessity to purify a corrupted or confused comprehension of prayer.

In our time, there are many issues to face in this regard. For many, prayer has been replaced altogether with pragmatism. Function overrides fellowship with God. Busyness crowds out communion. For others, prayer lacks a sense of awe and respect. It is flippant, disrespectful, irreverent. For others, it is demanding, claiming, attempting to force God by some ill-purposed faith to do what He has to do for us. For others, it is routine, ritual, formula.

The Disciples' Prayer resolves all the confusion and brings to us the fullness of prayer perspective from our Lord Himself.

One of the marvels of the infinite mind of God is His ability to speak of vast themes in few words. A few, aptly chosen terms have become the source of numberless books and sermons, songs and lessons that build upon one another as they stretch through the centuries of redemptive history.

What God can say in the economy of words that only His supernatural intelligence could select, provides insight into truth that man finds inexhaustible. Ages of study in the words of Scripture has not found the fullness of all that our Lord was saying.

Nowhere is that wonder more obvious than in the sixty-six words of the Disciples' Prayer in Matthew 6. Everything every man ever needed to understand prayer is latent in the choice disclosure of those words. That may sound like an astounding claim, but it is true. No set of volumes, no exhaustive thesis of great length, no series of teachings or preachings offered by men could ever have captured the fullness of all that prayer is, and is to be, as does that profoundly simple model.

It sets the standard for all praying. It encompasses all elements in prayer. It is for you, to change your praying—and more, to change your life.

1

The Purpose of Prayer

For too many people, the Disciples' Prayer—more commonly known as the Lord's Prayer—is simply something they have recited for years:

"Our Father, which art in heaven, Hallowed be thy name. Thy kingdom come. Thy will be done in earth, as it is in heaven. Give us this day our daily bread. And forgive us our debts as we forgive our debtors. And lead us not into temptation, but deliver us from evil: For thine is the kingdom, and the power, and the glory, for ever. Amen" (Matthew 6:9-13).

Yet in this tremendous portion of Scripture we face unequaled instruction regarding one of the most vital subjects in all of the Christian life—prayer. Much discussed, much taught, much written about, the topic may seem overworked, but it is still vital for all that has been said.

The believer must learn to pray to experience the fullness of communion with God, to open the floodgates of heaven. The apostle Paul said, "Pray without ceasing" (1 Thessalonians 5:17). Anything so consuming in Christian experience must be understood. If we do not know how to pray, or for what to pray, it does us little good to keep praying.

In this section of the Sermon on the Mount, Jesus the King gave the standards of His kingdom in contrast to the standards of the day. The Jews of Jesus' day had developed a system they thought was adequate to get them into the kingdom, but they were wrong— it was not. In Matthew 5, Jesus said their theology was not adequate. Later, in chapter 6, He would say their view of the material world was not adequate. But here He zeroed in on their religious activities. He told them that even their religious life fell short, and He focused on three areas: their giving, their praying, and their fasting.

Of the three, the greatest emphasis is on praying, because prayer is more important. To *give* properly, you must give only when your heart is filled with gratitude from the vitality of personal communion with God. And *fasting* is meaningless apart from prayer.

Martyn Lloyd-Jones, in *Studies in the Sermon on the Mount* (2 vols. [Grand Rapids: Eerdmans, 1977], 2:45) said, "Man is at his greatest and highest when upon his knees he comes face to face with God."

Jesus, then, was challenging the religion of His day. He said, in effect, "Your prayers, just like your giving and your fasting, are substandard."

But was He speaking only to the Old Testament-type Jews of His day? Are we not, in many, many cases, just as substandard and inadequate as they were? There is plenty of giving going on for self-glory, plenty of fasting to call attention to our supposed holiness, and plenty of praying that is a pretense, that does not recognize the basic biblical standards for true prayer. In fact, the apostle Paul said in Romans 8:26—and he said this about people on the same side of the cross we live on—"We know not what we should pray for as we ought. But the Spirit itself maketh intercession for us."

In other words, God is ever aiding our prayers because we do not know how to pray or for what to pray. Our Lord affirms the need for proper prayer in Matthew 6. There is not a lot of discussion here on how we are to give or how we are to fast. He mostly tells us how *not* to do those. But how we are to *pray* is specifically and comprehensively covered in this one simple prayer of sixty-six words.

It is an absolute masterpiece of God's infinite wisdom to somehow encompass every conceivable element in prayer and reduce it to one simple pattern. This particular pattern for prayer staggers my mind, and the longer I study it, the more I realize that there are infinite numbers of ways to view it.

I believe prayer is one of the two ultimate tests of true spirituality. The other is the study of the Word of God. Those are the avenues of spiritual communion between the believer and his Lord.

I believe—and I think the Bible supports this—that the study of the Word of God comes first. Why? Because we will not even know how to pray unless we know about God, His will, and what He says about our lives and our problems. Studying God's Word gives birth to a meaningful prayer life.

There are people who plead with God to give them the Holy Spirit, when the Bible says they already have the Holy Spirit (Romans 8:9; 1 Corinthians 12:13).

People plead with Christ for strength when the Bible says you can do all things through Christ who strengthens you (Philippians 4:13).

People pray, "Lord, be with us," and the Bible says, "Lo, I am with you always" (Matthew 28:20).

People plead for love for others; the Bible says,

"The love of God is shed abroad in our hearts" (Romans 5:5). You don't need to get it, you need to let it out.

Unless we understand the truth of the Word of God, we do not really know how to pray. When we study God's Word and discover His truth, we discover also the real condition of our hearts, the truth about our spiritual lives. Such discovery should drive us into opening our hearts to God.

Our Lord knew the place of prayer. The Bible says Jesus would rise a great while before dawn and go into the mountain to pray. In the evenings He went down the slope of the backside of Jerusalem across the Kidron brook, ascended the Mount of Olives, and there communed with the Father, sometimes all night long.

When Christ said, in Matthew 6:9, "After this manner, therefore, pray ye," He spoke out of personal involvement.

That teaching came at a marvelous time in the midst of the King's manifesto. It set for all time the understanding that prayer is vital to a kingdom citizen. It must have hit the Jews hard, because they had given priority to prayer. God had given them the purity of genuine prayer, but they had abandoned it for the routine and the ritual of empty religious exercises. They had their pet formulas, their "prayers" to be used at set times, but they did not communicate with God.

Actually, this New Testament prayer is simply a reaffirmation of something very old, which fits the thrust of the Sermon on the Mount. Jesus started the discourse by saying, in effect, "I didn't come to take anything away from the Old Testament or to add anything to it. In fact, not one jot or tittle shall be removed from that law."

When it came to prayer, He spoke of things they should have known and should have been incorporating already. If you know anything of the historic Jewish perspective on prayer, you know that Old Testament Jews believed they had a right to pray. A right to come to God was a major part of their life experience. They desired to come to God because they believed God wanted them there.

They did not come to God like pagans, in fear and trembling. The rabbis said, "The Holy One yearns for the prayers of the righteous."

Psalm 145:18 says, "The LORD is nigh unto all them that call upon him."

Psalm 91:15 says, "He shall call upon me, and I will answer him."

The Word of God makes clear that God wanted to hear their heart's cry. No true Jew with a right spirit ever doubted God's priority for prayer. The rabbis believed prayer was not just communication but also a mighty weapon that released God's power.

The *Midrash*, a Jewish commentary on some sections of the Old Testament, says this: "A human king can hearken to two or three people at one time, but he cannot hearken to more. God is not so. For all men may pray to Him and He hearkens to them all simultaneously. Men's ears become satisfied with hearing but God's ears are never satisfied; He is never wearied by men's prayers."

The Jewish teachers went even further, teaching that prayer was to be constant. They were trying to teach people to avoid the habit of praying only when they were desperate. Some people think prayer is like a parachute; they're glad it's there, but they hope they never have to use it.

The Talmud says, "Honor the physician before

you have need of him." And, "The Holy One says, 'Just as it is My office to cause the rain and the dew to fall and make the plants to grow and sustain man, so art thou bound to pray before Me and to praise Me in accordance with My works. Thou shalt not say, 'I am in prosperity—why should I pray,' but before misfortune comes, anticipate and pray."

So the Jews were right on the mark—they had the true perspective.

They also believed that prayers should incorporate certain elements:

• Loving praise. The psalmist says (Psalm 34:2), "I will bless the LORD at all times; his praise shall continually be in my mouth." Psalm 51:15 says, "O LORD, open thou my lips; and my mouth shall shew forth thy praise."

• Gratitude and thanksgiving. Jonah said, "I will sacrifice unto thee with the voice of thanksgiving" (Jonah 2:9). When the day comes that we have no more to ask for, we will have everything to be thankful for.

• A sense of awe, a sense of reverence for God's holiness. They did not treat God as if He were a man. They went to God realizing that when they entered into prayer, they came face to face with Him. When Isaiah came into the presence of God in holy awe, all he could say was, "I am a man of unclean lips, and I dwell in the midst of a people of unclean lips: for mine eyes have seen the King, the LORD of hosts" (Isaiah 6:5).

• A patent desire to obey God. One did not pray unless one's heart was really right. The whole of Psalm 119 affirms that over and over. "My tongue shall speak of thy word: for all thy commandments are righteous" (v. 172). There were no reservations in the heart of a true Jew; he went with a spirit of obedience, desiring to please God.

• Confession of sin. The Jews knew they were unclean in God's presence, as Isaiah said. David so many times had to get his sins straightened out before he could ever experience the fullness of God's presence. In Psalm 26:6, a wonderful verse, he says, "I will wash mine hands in innocency: so will I compass [go about] thine altar, O LORD." "Who shall ascend into the hill [presence] of the LORD? or who shall stand in His holy place? He that hath clean hands, and a pure heart" (Psalm 24:3-4).

• Unselfishness. The Jews had a sense of community that we don't really understand. They were national, a theocracy ruled by God. The very fact that Israel still exists as a nation shows how vitally they have clung to the preservation of that national identity.

Theirs were prayers that encompassed the whole; they were not isolated to the individual. For example, the rabbis had a very interesting prayer: "Hear not, O Lord, the prayer of the traveler."

The traveler might pray for good weather, accommodating skies, an easy journey. The rabbis were saying, "Lord, don't hear that prayer, because that's one guy on one trip praying for a fair day, when everyone else in that part of the world knows their crops need rain."

Most of us come to the Lord with a lot of "I, I, I, me, me, me, my, my, my." We do not know what it is to encompass the whole body. Sometimes we have to sacrifice what seems best for ourselves because God has a greater plan for the whole.

You find no singular personal pronouns in the Lord's Prayer. It says, "Our Father . . . our daily bread . . . our debts . . . our debtors." Prayer is to be unselfish.

• Perseverance. They did not give up. After the children of Israel had worshiped the golden calf, the Bible tells us, Moses prayed for forty days in a row that God would forgive them. That's perseverance.

• Humility. A true Jew came to prayer to submit himself to the will of God. The greatest illustration of that came from the heart of the truest Jew who ever lived. It is the prayer of the Lord Jesus in the garden: "Nevertheless not my will, but thine, be done" (Luke 22:42).

Prayer is not asking God to do *my* will. It is bringing myself into conformity with *His* will. It is asking Him to do His will and to give me the grace to enjoy it.

All those elements were part of the traditional prayer life of a true Jew. The Jews had a great heritage of genuine prayer.

But something went wrong. Jewish prayer became hypocritical. Our Lord says they prayed "to be seen by men" (Matthew 6:5).

He was saying in effect, "They're phonies. They are not talking to Me anymore. They're selfish [verse 7]. They're trying to gain things for their own ends. They're making a public display. They go on with vain babblings and repetitions like pagan people, thinking that I'm going to do something just because I'm so sick of hearing them that I'll do it to shut them up. And then they have the unimaginable pride [Matthew 6:8] to think they need to inform Me about things."

So what you have in the next five verses in Matthew 6 is really Jesus' reiterating the ingredients of prayer from Old Testament Jewish tradition. Although everything He says adds richness, and He takes it further than it has ever gone, He does not really say anything totally new.

We need that teaching today because we do not know how to pray much better than they did. We especially miss the point when we take this prayer and just repeat it. People may say, "Well, we believe it's a prayer to be recited." No, it is not. It's fine to recite it, just as it is fine to read any part of the Bible. But it is *not* just a prayer to be recited.

Why?

Number one, this prayer is recorded twice in Scripture (here in Matthew 6 and again in Luke 11), and the wording differs somewhat. If the Lord was giving us a prayer to be memorized and recited, He would not have given us different words the two times He gave it.

Second, in Luke 11 they said, "Teach us *to pray.*" They did not say, "Teach us *a prayer.*" It is one thing to read a prayer; it's something else to know how to pray.

Matthew 6:7 says, "But when ye pray, use not vain repetitions, as the heathen." Would He then immediately follow by giving us a prayer to repeat? Ridiculous.

There is no occasion in the entire New Testament on which this prayer is ever repeated by anybody else. It is a model, a skeleton upon which to put flesh.

This prayer covers everything and can be looked at from so many angles that it's mind-boggling. If you concentrate on the Disciples' Prayer and work your way through its outline, no matter what you are praying about, you will have the confidence that you're praying the way Jesus taught.

For example, one of many ways to look at this prayer is in how it unfolds the relationship we have with God. Notice:

"Our Father" means we have a father/child relationship with God.

"Hallowed be thy name" means we have a deity/worshiper relationship with God.

"Thy kingdom come" says we have a sovereign/subject relationship.

"Thy will be done" says we have a master/servant relationship.

"Give us our daily bread" means we have a benefactor/beneficiary relationship.

"Forgive us our trespasses, or debts" means we have a Savior/sinner relationship.

"Lead us not into temptation" says we have a guide/pilgrim relationship.

The prayer also defines the spirit in which we are to pray. "Our" reflects an unselfish spirit; "Father," a family spirit; "hallowed be thy name," a reverent spirit; "thy kingdom come," a loyal spirit; "thy will be done," a submissive spirit; "give us . . . our daily bread," a dependent spirit; "forgive us," a penitent spirit; "lead us not into temptation," a humble spirit; "thine is the kingdom," a triumphant spirit; "and the glory," an exultant spirit; "forever," an eternal spirit.

The prayer can be divided into two sets of three elements each. The first three (hallowed be thy name, thy kingdom come, thy will be done) deal with God's glory. The second three (give us our daily bread, forgive us our debts, lead us not into temptation) deal with man's need.

When you pray, you set God in His rightful place, and everything else flows from there. All prayer is to begin with the character of God. When God is first, prayer makes sense.

Another angle: The purpose of prayer, number one, is to hallow the name of God. Number two, to bring in His kingdom. Number three, to do His will.

What are the means by which His name is hallowed, His kingdom lifted up, and His will done? First, by giving us our daily bread (provision); second, by forgiving our sins (pardon); third, by leading us not into temptation (protection).

We can also look at this prayer and see God first as Father (hallowed be the Father's name), then as King (His kingdom comes), then as Master (His will is done).

The elements, the wonders, the beauties of this model of prayer are almost infinite. Only the mind of God could have conceived such far-reaching, incredible thoughts compressed into this tiny section of Scripture. Let me show you even more approaches to it:

"Our daily bread" is the present.

"Our debts" are sins from the past.

"And lead us not . . ." is the future.

Bread is physical; forgiveness is mental (relieving the anguish of guilt); and temptation is spiritual.

There is even alliteration, and not just for a good outline. "Our Father" indicates God's paternity. "Hallowed" shows His priority. "Thy kingdom" is His program. "Thy will" is His purpose. "Our bread" is His provision. "Forgive us" is His pardon. "And lead us not" is His protection. "For thine is the kingdom, and the power, and the glory, for ever" is His preeminence.

If you think prayer is for your benefit, you've missed the point. That's why we get so confused: we're praying for ourselves (see James 4:3). The reason we pray and the reason God answers is to put Himself and His glory on display. His glory is the issue. That is the message of John 14:13: "What-

soever ye shall ask in my name, that will I do, that
the Father may be glorified."

Your prayer will not force God. You cannot
badger Him, irritate Him, "con" Him. You can only
submit to His sovereignty and seek His glory.

That is the affirmation of the Disciple's Prayer.

2

"Our Father"—
The Paternity of Prayer

If prayer is something we are to do unceasingly, then we had better know how to do it properly. So our Lord teaches us to pray.

Notice what He *does not* teach us:

He does not teach us the *posture* of prayer, because any posture will do. In the Bible, people prayed standing, lifting their hands, sitting, lying down, kneeling, lifting their eyes, bowing, placing their heads between their knees, pounding their chests, and facing a temple.

He does not teach us the *place* to pray. People in the Bible prayed during battle, in a cave, in a closet, in a garden, on a mountainside, by a river, by the sea, in the street, in God's house, in hades, in bed, in a home, in a fish, on a housetop, in a prison, in solitude, in the wilderness, and on a cross.

First Timothy 2:8 says, "I will . . . that men pray every where."

Jesus does not tell us *when* to pray. In the Bible people are found praying in the early morning, midmorning, three times a day, in the evening, before meals, after meals, at the ninth hour, at bedtime, at midnight, day and night, today, often, when they're young, when they're old, in trouble, every day, and always.

Neither did Jesus say what to wear or how to act while praying. Biblical petitioners sometimes wore sackcloth, sat in ashes, shaved their heads, cried out, applied dust to their heads, tore their garments, fasted, sighed, groaned, wept, sweat blood, agonized with broken hearts and broken spirits, poured out their hearts, made oaths, offered sacrifices, offered praise, and sang.

In any posture, at any time, in any place, under any circumstances, in any attire—prayer is fitting. Sometimes it becomes more concentrated and intense than at other times, but prayer is to be a way of life. As we saw in John 14:13-14, our dear Lord says that when we ask anything in His name, He hears us, "that the Father may be glorified."

Even in the deepest, most severe circumstance, even in pits of despair we could hardly imagine, the true saints of God in the Old Testament would worship God in prayer. Jonah was in the belly of a great fish. Talk about fear; talk about misery! He began a prayer in Jonah 2 that makes you wonder if he knew where he was. You would think he'd just say, "Get me out of here, God."

But Jonah began with a marvelous anthem of worship and praise, because he knew that no man can really ask God for something unless he first affirms that God has the sovereign right to say yes or no.

Daniel was constantly on the precipice of disaster because of his strategic place in the pagan Babylonian society (Daniel 9). He bowed to pray in the midst of a terrible situation and uttered a prayer that almost ignored his situation and proclaimed the majesty, glory, dignity, holiness, and the almighty character of sovereign God.

Jeremiah (in Jeremiah 32), who spent most of his life in frustration and confusion, weeping with a broken heart over his people, poured out a prayer in the midst of his perplexity, and it is nothing less than a recitation of God's majesty, attribute after attribute.

Why did the Old Testament saints do that? And why does the Disciples' Prayer begin, "Our Father, which art in heaven, Hallowed be thy name. Thy kingdom come. Thy will be done"? And why does it end, "For thine is the kingdom, and the power, and the glory, for ever"? Because God is the focus of all prayer.

In Psalm 86 David was about to seek God's mercy, love, compassion, and tenderness in his own behalf. Beginning in verse 6 he said, "Give ear, O LORD, unto my prayer; and attend to the voice of my supplications. In the day of my trouble I will call upon thee: for thou wilt answer me."

He was in the midst of trouble, his heart was burdened, there was tremendous anxiety in his spirit. But he quickly shifted gears in verse 8: "Among the gods there is none like unto thee, O LORD." He did not begin with a specific petition, but rather with an affirmation of the majesty and the character of God. He extolled God for who He was and what He had done:

"All nations whom thou hast made shall come and worship before thee, O LORD; and shall glorify thy name. . . . For thou art great, and doest wondrous things: thou art God alone."

That is the typical prayer of the Old Testament saint who knew what prayer was all about—that it meant setting God in His rightful place and then bringing our wills into submission to His. That's

exactly what David did beautifully in verse 11:
"Teach me thy way, O LORD; I will walk in thy
truth."

Let's stop there. Notice he did not even mention
yet the request in his heart. He simply said, "I want
to acknowledge that You are God and You have a
right to do what You want, and second, I submit to
Your way and Your will." Then comes this magnifi-
cent statement at the end of verse 11: "Unite my
heart to fear thy name."

Make my heart one with Your heart! That is
prayer!

Then in verse 12 he wrote that no matter what
happened, "I will praise thee, O LORD my God,
with all my heart: and I will glorify thy name for
evermore."

Now with that in mind, let's go back to Matthew
6 and look again at how every facet, every short,
power-packed statement in this prayer focuses on
God. It begins by calling on God.

"Father" is probably the most common term we
use in prayer, and rightly so, for that is the pattern
Jesus set. Prayer should always begin with the recognition that God is our Father.

God is our Father. What a tremendous truth. The
word "our" refers to believing people, a fact that is
a death blow to the liberal teaching of the fatherhood of God and the brotherhood of man.

For years, liberals have taught that God is everybody's Father, so we're all the children of God and
thus all brothers. But the only sense in which that
is true is the sense of creation. Malachi 2:10 says,
"Have we not all one father? hath not one God
created us?" In Acts 17:29 Paul said, "We are the
offspring of God."

In the sense of creation, yes, God is our Father.

In the sense of familial relationship, He is not.

Jesus said in John 8:44 to the Jewish leaders, "Ye are of your father the devil."

First John 3 clearly characterizes two families: the children of God and the children of the devil. The former do not continue to commit sin; the latter do.

The apostle Paul made a clear distinction between children of light and children of darkness. There is simply not just one spiritual family of mankind under one universal fatherhood of God. Second Peter 1:4 says that only those who believe have been made "partakers of the divine nature."

To "as many as *received* him," He gave the right to be called the sons of God, says John 1:12 (italics added).

So Jesus' very statement *"Our* Father" eliminates a world of unbelieving people.

On the positive side, "Our Father" declares a wondrous intimacy with God. Most of the world at that time worshiped gods that were distant, remote, fearful beings. Unfortunately there was even an amazing remoteness in the Jewish thinking of Jesus' day. The Old Testament Jew understood God's fatherhood more in terms of His overall care of the nation Israel than in terms of the intimate relationship He offered.

To them, God became more and more remote as they moved away from true religion and even stopped using God's name. It became blasphemous even to mention the name of Yahweh. They had developed a wide gulf, so when Jesus uttered the term "Our Father," it was shocking to them. It awakened in them something lost long ago.

But they *had* once had it. In Isaiah 64, the people of Israel had sinned grossly. Verses 6-7 say, "We are all as an unclean thing, and all our righteousnesses are as filthy rags; and we all do fade as a leaf; and our iniquities, like the wind, have taken us away.

"And there is none that calleth upon thy name, that stirreth up himself to take hold of thee: for thou hast hid thy face from us, and hast consumed us, because of our iniquities."

That's a desperate situation. To what does Isaiah then appeal? Verse 8 beautifully says, "But now, O LORD, thou art our father." Isaiah reminded them of the comforting reality that fathers take care of their children.

The Jews in the Old Testament saw five basic things in the fatherhood of God:

• First, God was a Father in terms of His begetting. First Chronicles 29:10 gives Him a title—"LORD God of Israel, our Father"—the one who has begotten the nation.

• Second, the Jews saw the nearness of God. A father is closer than an uncle or a cousin or a friend or a neighbor. Psalm 68 provides a good illustration of this, with a discussion of God and His power. It speaks of God's riding the clouds and of His twenty thousand chariots and angels. God is flying through the sky and ascending great mounts of holiness, and then the narrative pulls back from all that grandeur and says simply: "A father to the fatherless." Isn't that great?

• Third, the Jews saw His loving grace. A father is forgiving, tenderhearted, merciful, and gracious, and thus it is said in Psalm 103:13, "As a father pitieth his children, so the LORD pitieth them that fear him."

• Fourth, I believe the Jews of the Old Testament saw the fatherhood of God in terms of His guidance. Jeremiah 31:9 says, "They shall come with weeping, and with supplications will I lead them: I will cause them to walk by the rivers of waters in a straight way, wherein they shall not stumble: [Why?] for I am a father to Israel."

But none of that sentimentalized God to them, because they saw another element.

• Fifth, they had to see that because God was their Father, they were required to obey Him, A simple statement in Deuteronomy 32:6 reiterates that: "Do ye thus requite the LORD, O foolish people and unwise? Is not he thy father that hath bought thee?"

They understood God as a Father; begetting, loving, living alongside, guiding, and training them in obedience. And they knew they were responsible to obey. That was the true Jewish concept.

Now read Matthew 7:7: "Ask, and it shall be given you; seek, and ye shall find; knock, and it shall be opened unto you: For every one that asketh receiveth; and he that seeketh findeth; and to him that knocketh it shall be opened."

Why? Why was God going to do that? Verse 9 says: "What man is there of you, whom if his son ask bread, will he give him a stone? Or if he ask a fish, will he give him a serpent? If ye then, being evil, know how to give good gifts unto your children, how much more shall your Father which is in heaven give good things to them that ask him?"

The Jews were again introduced to the fact that God is a beneficent, caring, loving, sustaining Father, but they had long since lost a sense of intimacy with Him.

Perhaps the fact that the Greeks of that time called their gods "father" left the Pharisees and the scribes thinking that God as a father was an empty thought meaning no more than a god, or a ruler, or a king.

Two major philosophies existed at the time of Christ in the Greek and Roman worlds. The Stoics said the major attribute of a god is *apatheia*, the essential inability to experience any feeling. They had decided that since a person who can feel love can also be hurt, and a person who can feel joy can also feel sadness, the gods must not feel anything. The Stoics chose therefore to be passionless, emotionless, incapable of any feeling, apathetic, and indifferent.

The Epicureans, on the other hand, had the idea that the supreme quality of the deities was *ataraxia*, which means serenity, complete calm, perfect peace. They felt that if the gods got involved in human affairs, they would lose their calm. Therefore, the gods were detached.

The Stoics said the gods were apathetic and indifferent; the Epicureans said the gods were uninterested and isolated. Though they used the term *father* for some of their gods, still they attributed those character traits of impotence to them.

Then Jesus came along and used the term *Father* in a new fashion, injecting into it something rich and special and intimate. Jesus made intimacy with God a possibility.

When Jesus prayed, He used the word *Father*, in fact, more than seventy times. The only prayer He ever prayed without using it was when He was on the cross. "My God, my God, why hast thou forsaken me?" Only in sin-bearing was He separated from the Father.

When you pray, "Father," you are not talking about Father Goose or Father Nature or some beneficent character who wants to drop golden eggs on you. Such a title is not a reference to some deity totally unconcerned, a father only in a leadership or headship sense. You are talking about someone who is also loving, personally involved, and absolutely intimate.

How does modern man see the God who would be intimate? Poet Thomas Hardy wrote that prayer was useless because there was no one to pray to except, "that dreaming, dark, dumb thing that turns the handle of this idle show" (cited in William Barclay, *The Beautitudes and the Lord's Prayer for Every Man* [New York: Harper & Row, 1963], p. 168).

The Stoics' god was emotionless, the Epicureans' utterly detached, the modern philosophers' dark, dreaming, and silent. Even the Jews of Jesus' time saw God as a father only in their remote, faded past with little meaning.

To all of that confusion Jesus simply uttered—without explanation—two words, "Our Father." In so doing He cracked open a shell that empties upon us marvelous new dimensions of meaning.

The Greek term is *pater*. Jesus did not use that term. He spoke Aramaic although the Bible was written in Greek. There is little doubt in my mind that He used the term *Abba*, for Abba was the familiar, endearing term used by a child for its father. It means daddy.

Romans 8:15 and Galatians 4:6 say that we can cry, "Abba, Father." We do not see God the way the Jews used to see Him, as just some deity responsible for the nation. We don't come to Him as some indifferent, detached ideal. We come to God as our intimate Father.

What does it mean that God is our Father?

First, it means the end of fear. Missionaries tell us that one of the greatest gifts Christianity ever brings to heathen societies is the certainty that God is a loving, caring Father, because heathen people live under the fear of their gods.

Their worlds are literally jammed full of gods that are jealous, hostile, grudging, and vengeance-prone, and of whom they live in terror.

That is why it's so wonderful when Jesus says, "Our Father." You don't have to fear God; He's your Father through Christ.

Second, God as a Father settles the matter of hope. In the midst of a hostile world that's falling apart, God is our Father, and He'll take care of our future, our destiny.

Third, it means the end of loneliness, bitterness, the loss of self-worth, despair. We all suffer self-pity; we desperately need respect. Where are we going to get it? Is there anybody who knows us for what we are and loves us anyway? Is there anyone who can lift us up and give us value? Can anybody make us feel we have a friend?

God can. He's our Father. He is with us always. He's a friend that sticks closer than a brother.

Fourth, I think "our Father" settles the matter of selfishness. He's not "my Father." He's "ours." Prayer should embrace the community of faith. The very use of the word *our* ends all claims to exclusivity.

Fifth, God as a Father settles the matter of resources, because Christ says, "Our Father, which art in heaven." That means He is not drawing resources from the world. He's drawing from heaven. He has all the supernatural domain at His disposal.

All that heaven is, and all that it means (see Ephesians) to be blessed in the heavenlies with all spiritual blessing, is available in Him.

If you want satisfaction, God has it at His disposal.

If you want fairness, God has it in the heavenlies.

Peace, fellowship, knowledge, victory, boldness? It is all there. I pray to a Father who has eternal resources. What a thought!

Sixth, seeing God as a Father settles the matter of obedience. My children are to obey me although I am an unworthy father. We are to obey Him, and He is an infinitely worthy Father.

Obedience is an essential element in the concept of the fatherhood of God. Jesus obeyed the Father. He said, "I came . . . not to do mine own will, but the will of him that sent me." He said, "My meat is to do the will of him that sent me." And, "Nevertheless not my will, but thine be done."

If He could assign Himself a place of subservience in perfection, certainly we can be subservient in our imperfection.

Finally, it settles the matter of wisdom. If God is a father, then He is infinitely wiser than we are.

What happens when you know God is your Father? It removes fear, it provides hope, it ends loneliness, it does away with selfishness, it provides heavenly resources, it demands obedience, and it declares wisdom.

To begin a prayer, "Our Father, which art in heaven," is to indicate eagerness to come as a child, beloved by a Father, to receive all that His love and eternal, supernatural resources can possibly give.

3

"Hallowed Be Thy Name"—
The Priority of Prayer

"A monarch vested in gorgeous habiliments is far
less illustrious than a kneeling supplicant ennobled
and adorned by communion with his God. Consider how august a privilege it is when angels are
present and archangels throng around where
cherubim and seraphim encircle with their blaze
the throne of God, that a mortal may approach
with unrestrained confidence and converse with
heaven's dread sovereign. O what honor was ever
conferred like that? [Chrysostom]

Imagine entering the very throne room and
communing with the living God of the universe.
You may get an idea of a gift so marvelous that it
should be sufficient to draw us to pray constantly.

But prayer is more than just the privilege of
communing with God. Prayer gives God a vehicle
by which He can demonstrate who He is.
Jesus said, "Whatsoever ye shall ask in my name,
that will I do, that the Father may be glorified in the
Son" (John 14:13).

Prayer is ever and always, first and foremost, a
recognition of God's majestic glory and an act of
submission to it. All our petitions, all our passions,
all our supplications, all our requests, all our needs,

all our trials, all our problems are subject to His
name (Matthew 6:9), His kingdom, and His will (v.
10).

Then God gives (v. 11), forgives (v. 12), and leads
us (v. 13). But that comes only when we put God
first. True worship begins with God, forgets self,
and glorifies Him.

There is a movement afoot in the church today in
which people are staking claims on what they believe God has to do; going into His presence an-
nouncing that He "must" do this or that. I've heard
three individuals on television who tell people to
demand things from God, by faith. One says that if
you are a spirit-filled Christian you should never
know a day of illness in your life. You demand by
faith that God keep you well. It is your right, they
say.

Demanding things from God on your own conditions is a theologically errant but common approach to prayer run rampant. And whether we
like to admit it, in many cases that's the way we
pray.

To see how old that kind of praying is, look at
Genesis 28:20. "And Jacob vowed a vow, saying, If
God will be with me, and will keep me in this way
that I go, and will give me bread to eat, and raiment
to put on, so that I come again to my father's house
in peace; then shall the LORD by my God."

How's that for a conditional prayer? God, do you
want me on Your side? Fork over the following!

"And this stone, which I have set for a pillar,
shall be God's house: and of all that thou shalt give
me I will surely give the tenth unto thee."

That was not a spiritual vow; it was carnal. We
don't have to badger God. We don't have to bang
away and do special things to get Him to respond.

We're not like the prophets and priests of Baal (1 Kings 18:20-29).

Our God *does* care and is *not* asleep. He is there waiting for us to enter His presence, because He's a loving Father who cares for His children, whatever their circumstance.

Paul Tournier, the great Christian doctor, wrote in his *Doctor's Case Book*, "There was one patient of mine, the youngest daughter in a large family which the father found it difficult to support. One day she heard her father mutter despairingly, referring to her, 'We could well have done without that one.' That is precisely what God can never say. He is a loving Father to every one of His children" (cited in William Barclay, *The Beatitudes and the Lord's Prayer for Every Man* [New York: Harper & Row, 1963], p. 172).

God told Moses, "I know thee by name" (Exodus 33:12, 17).

Do you ever wonder why God bothered with all those names in the seemingly endless genealogies of Scripture? Whatever His specific purpose, I think one reason is that God wanted people to know that He knows each of us by name.

Later in the Sermon on the Mount comes Christ's wonderful statement that not one sparrow falls without our Father's knowing it. If you take that out of the Greek and put it in Aramaic—which Christ spoke—it says that not one sparrow *hops* without our Father's knowing it. He does not just know when a sparrow dies, but He also knows where a sparrow lights when it hops!

Because of the unconditional love of God as a Father, we want to give Him His proper priority. In the phrase in Matthew 6:9 "Hallowed be thy name," we see the first petition in the prayer. And it is on God's behalf.

Arthur W. Pink says, "How clearly then is the fundamental duty of prayer set forth. Self and all its needs must be given a secondary place, and the Lord freely accorded the pre-eminence in our thoughts and supplications. This petition must take the precedence, for the glory of God's great name is the ultimate end of all things." (*An Exposition of the Sermon on the Mount* [Grand Rapids: Baker, 1950], pp. 161-62.)

Even though He is my loving Father, even though He cares to meet my needs, and even though He has heavenly resources to do that, my first petition is not on my own behalf, but on His. "Hallowed be thy name" is a warning against self-seeking prayer.

What is implied in its meaning? Is it just an epithet attached as a passing homage to God? I think not. When Jesus says, "Hallowed be thy name," He says something so full and rich that one could never exhaust what it means in this or any other body of writing.

It encompasses all of God's nature and all of man's response to His nature. It isn't religious routine or just a nice thought about God. It opens up a whole dimension of respect, reverence, awe, appreciation, honor, glory, adoration, and worship.

Though they thought little of dishonoring His person, the Jews had attached such a sacredness to God's name that they would not say it aloud. They tried to hallow the name itself, but they disobeyed His Word and destroyed His truths.

There is no such word as *Jehovah* in Hebrew. Although it appears throughout the English language Old Testament, there's no such word. The name of God in Exodus 3:14, where He said, "I AM THAT I AM," is *Yahweh*. The other familiar name for God is

Adonai, which means the Lord God.

The Jews would not say *Yahweh*. Eventually the consonants were taken out of *Yahweh*, the vowels out of Adonai, and put together to form "Jehovah," really a non-word. That was done to avoid having to say the real word, but what a superficiality!

What the Lord is teaching us here in hallowing the name is not some mystical attitude toward the term *God*, but that we respect God for who He is. It is an all-encompassing concept. The Jews should have known better, because in Old Testament times, names were more than titles.

First Samuel 18:30 says, "Then the princes of the Philistines went forth: and it came to pass, after they went forth, that David behaved himself more wisely than all the servants of Saul; so that his name was much set by [esteemed]."

They were not esteeming the letters in his name. The fact that his name was esteemed meant he himself was esteemed. We say today, "So-and-so has made a name for himself; so-and-so has a good name." We mean that there is something about his character worthy of our praise.

In Scripture, the name stood for the whole character of the person. In Exodus 34:6-7 God says, "The LORD, the LORD God, merciful and gracious, longsuffering, and abundant in goodness and truth, keeping mercy for thousands, forgiving iniquity and transgression and sin." In other words, the name of God is the composite of all His attributes.

Hallowing His name does not mean having some kind of fetish about not speaking it aloud. It is hallowing all that God is, which is embodied in His name. Psalm 9:10 says, "They that know thy name will put their trust in thee."

Does everyone who knows the word *God* trust in Him? Of course not. But those who perceive the fullness of who He is trust in Him. When the blinders come off and you see God for who He is, you will trust Him.

Psalm 7:17 says, "I will praise the LORD according to his righteousness: and will sing praise to the name of the LORD most high."

Psalm 102:15 says, "So the heathen shall fear the name of the LORD." Did they fear the letters in the word? Of course not. They feared the Lord God Himself.

In plain terms, then, we might begin the Disciples' Prayer this way: "Our Father, who loves us and cares for us, and who has in heaven supplies to meet our every need; may Your person, Your identity, Your character, Your nature, Your attributes, Your reputation, Your very being itself be hallowed."

This is not, then, some glib phrase thrown at God periodically in a ritual. This is a way of approaching God continuously.

God is given many names in the Bible, and each expresses some part of His character. In Genesis He is called *Elohim*, the "Creator God." Later in the same book He is called *El Elyon*, or "possessor of heaven and earth."

The Old Testament also calls Him: *Jehovah-Jireh*, "the Lord will provide"; *Jehovah-Nissi*, "the Lord our banner"; *Jehovah-Rapha*, "the Lord that healeth"; *Jehovah-Shalom*, "the Lord our peace"; *Jehovah-Raah*, "the Lord our Shepherd"; *Jehovah-Tsidkenu*, "the Lord our righteousness"; *Jehovah-Sabaoth*, "the Lord of hosts"; *Jehovah-Shama*, "the Lord is present and near"; and *Jehovah-Maqodeshkim*, which means "the Lord sanctifieth thee."

The Bible calls Him by all those terms to show
the fullness of who He is. But the greatest name by
which God has ever been designated in history is
the name of the Lord Jesus Christ, which means
Savior, and Master, and King.

And as the Lord Jesus Christ, God drew to Himself many other names: the Bread of Life, the Living Water, the Way, the Truth, the Life, the Resur-
rection, the Good Shepherd, the Branch, the
Bright and Morning Star, the Lamb of God, the
Rose of Sharon, the Lily of the Valley, the Door,
and on and on.

Even the Old Testament (Isaiah 9) gives names
for Christ: "Wonderful, Counselor, the Mighty
God, the Prince of Peace, the Everlasting Father,"
all designations of His nature.

That is why Romans 1:5 says they preached the
gospel that the nations might believe, for the sake
of His name.

Third John 7 says, "For *his name's sake* they went
forth" (italics added).

What does it mean to hallow? It makes us think
of cloistered halls, ivy-covered walls, long robes,
dismal chants, halos, musty dim churches, mourn-
ful music, and other tired traditions. "Hallowed" is
an archaic word, granted. Translators of the various
versions of the Bible have kept it because of its
familiarity, but let me tell you what it means.

It comes from a Greek verb *hagiazo,* a very important word in the Bible. The noun form, *hagios,*
means holy. It carries two basic ideas. The first can
mean to make an ordinary thing extraordinary by
bringing it into contact with something extraordinary. That's how it is used in 1 Peter 1:16, where
Peter says, "Be ye holy." It means that we're unholy, but by coming into contact with One who is
holy, we can be made holy.

Is that the meaning of "hallowed" in the Disciples' Prayer? No. We're not making God holy. In this reference it is meant to treat something or someone as sacred, to hold something or someone as set apart and holy, to regard someone as separated. We are simply petitioning that He be revered and regarded as holy.

So what does it mean to be holy? Holy means to be different. Not that everybody who is different is holy, but everybody who's holy is different.

God is called the Holy One because He is in a different sphere—He has a different quality of being. Leviticus 21:8 tells us that the priests were to be holy, to be different from other men. They were set apart to serve God.

God is uncommon, extraordinary, unearthly, separated from sinners, undefiled, the Bible says. He is holy.

We are to speak to God in reverence. In Numbers 20:11-12, after God had told Moses to merely speak, he smote the rock twice to draw water. God did not make the whole congregation pay for Moses' sin, so "water came out abundantly, and the congregation drank, and their beasts also. And the LORD spake unto Moses and Aaron, Because ye believed me not, to sanctify me [the same word in the Septuagint, *hagiazo*, one to be reverenced, honored, glorified, set apart, obeyed] in the eyes of the children of Israel, therefore ye shall not bring this congregation into the land which I have given them."

To hallow God's name means to hold His matchless being in reverence so that you will believe what He says and will obey Him.

I am deeply distressed by the current fads and flippancy that manifest the shallowness of much current Christianity. But nothing is more disturbing than a failure to recognize the most central truth about God—that He is holy, holy, holy (Isaiah 6:3)! The only one of His attributes thrice repeated is His holiness.

God's desire and demand for a proper recognition of His holiness are manifold in Scripture.

Moses and Aaron angrily struck the rock instead of speaking as God commanded, and thus they failed to treat God as holy in the sight of the sons of Israel. Neither of them entered the promised land.

Saul did not submit himself to the holiness of God as revealed by God's law. Rather, in impatience and self-styled disobedience, he failed to follow all of God's instructions (1 Samuel 15:11). So God removed him from the throne.

Uzzah failed to recognize the majesty of God's holiness in daring to defy God's instructions (Numbers 4:15, 19-20). God struck him down for his irreverence (2 Samuel 6:7).

Uzziah became proud, acted corruptly, was unfaithful to the Lord, and in an affront to God's holiness, entered the Temple to burn incense. God struck him with leprosy to the day of his death (2 Chronicles 26:16-23).

Ananias and Sapphira lied to the Holy Spirit. In sinning against the holiness of God, they lost their lives within hours (Acts 5:1-11).

The Corinthians ate of the bread and drank from the cup in an unholy manner (1 Corinthians 11:27-30). As a result, many were sick and some even died.

Now God does not always deal as immediately and directly in a physical way with those who fail to uphold His holy character. But there will always be an effect. Let's note some of them.

First, the enemy is given opportunity to blaspheme God. That is what Nathan told David (2 Samuel 12:14; cf. Ezekiel 20:39; 1 Timothy 5:14; 6:1).

Second, God's Word is dishonored (Titus 2:5).

Third, sin can disqualify you from further service in the King's court. Saul is the classic illustration (1 Samuel 15:23).

Fourth, life and well-being can be withdrawn (Acts 5:5, 10).

Fifth, spiritual blessings can be withheld (Numbers 20:12).

Sixth, God's anger is invoked (Isaiah 5:25).

Seventh, God's Spirit is grieved (Isaiah 63:10).

The psalmist asked rhetorically, "Who shall dwell in thy holy hill?" (Psalm 15:1-2). The answer is simply, "He that walketh uprightly, and worketh righteousness, and speaketh the truth in his heart." There is no greater need today than for church people to once again ascend the platform of fearing God.

"No religion has been greater than its idea of God." That gem from A. W. Tozer has a corollary. No church is greater than its reverent awe of a thrice holy God.

I think you can see this truth. God is holy and demands recognition as such. We can know that and yet not really perceive what that means practically.

Clearly, the fear of God is not optional. "Be thou in the fear of the LORD all the day long" (Proverbs 23:17). "Fear Him which is able to destroy both soul and body in hell" (Matthew 10:28). "Obey in all things . . . fearing God" (Colossians 3:22). "Fear God" (1 Peter 2:17).

Central to the book of Proverbs is the Hebrew word *yare*, which carries the idea of fear and honor. Solomon used it 18 times (1:7, 29; 2:5; 8:13; 9:10;

10:27; 13:13; 14:2, 16, 26, 27; 15:16, 33; 16:6; 19:23; 22:4; 23:17; 31:30).

The people of God have always been called to such a perspective of God's holy awesomeness. The fear of God pressed Manoah to expect instant death because he had seen God (Judges 13:22), and Job, repenting in the awesome presence of God's holiness, retracted all that he had foolishly said (Job 42:5-6).

Standing in the presence of God's holiness, Isaiah pronounced a curse on himself, "Woe is me for I am undone [ruined]!" (Isaiah 6:5), whereas Habakkuk trembled at the voice of a holy God (Habakkuk 3:16). The restored remnant feared the Lord when they heard His holy word spoken by the prophet Haggai (Haggai 1:12).

During the earthly ministry of our Savior, the disciples were afraid of the storm, but feared greatly (lit. "feared a great fear") when He calmed the storm (Mark 4:41). They were more afraid in recognizing the presence and power of God than they were of the deadly storm. They had an awe of God.

An unbelieving community begged Him to leave their region because they feared His holy power (Mark 5:17). They too were in awe of God's might.

Stained by the sin of unbelief, Peter implored his sinless Lord to depart from him (Luke 5:8). John, James, and Peter fell on their faces and were exceedingly afraid when they heard the voice of God (Matthew 17:6).

The Jerusalem church was deeply moved by the awe of a holy God (Acts 2:43; 5:5, 11). Throughout Judea, Galilee, and Samaria, the churches were going on in fear of the Lord (Acts 9:31).

Beholding the magnificence of the glorified

Christ, the beloved disciple fell in fear at His feet as a dead man (Revelation 1:17).

For each of those, the presence of God produced the "trauma of holiness." I believe such an attitude is largely missing in this method-oriented, pragmatic day. To revive it, those of us who stand in the place of the Lord to speak and lead must pursue holiness in the fear of God.

Moses urged Israel to respond to Creator holiness with creation holiness (Leviticus 11:44; 19:2). Peter echoed that plea. "But as he which hath called you is holy, so be ye holy in all manner of conversation; because it is written, Be ye holy; for I am holy" (1 Peter 1:15-16).

So the hour's challenge for Christ's church is this, "Let us cleanse ourselves from all filthiness of the flesh and spirit, perfecting holiness in the fear of God" (2 Corinthians 7:1).

John Calvin put it this way: "That God's name should be hallowed is to say that God should have His own honor of which He is so worthy, so that men should never think or speak of Him without the greatest veneration."

Too much "Our Father"—too much Abba, too much Daddy, turns into sentimentalism, and we could drag God down to a kind of buddy-buddy relationship. That is a problem in current Christianity right now. People talk to God in such low-level terms that they do not really do justice to His hallowed name. We've got the Father part down; but we think of God as the big Daddy who is going to give us everything we want.

I think that's why after "Our Father," Abba, He says, "Hallowed, holy, reverenced is Your name." True Old Testament Jews recognized that need, and their prayers always began, "O Lord, Father and

Ruler of my life"; "O Lord, Father and God of my life"; "O Father, King of great power, Most High and Almighty God."

The *Shmone 'esreh* is a set of eighteen prayers a Jew was to pray every day. Every prayer began, "O Father," "O King," or "O Lord." In the ten penitential days at the time of the Day of Atonement, the Jews prayed through what they called the *Avinu malkenu* forty-four times. They repeated, "Our Father, Our King, Our Father, Our King, Our Father, Our King," because they never wanted the concept of God to cause them to be sentimental about the majestic, sovereign King.

First Peter 3:15 says, "Sanctify the Lord God in your hearts." He uses the same word, *hagiazon.*

Even Jesus desired that the Father's name be honored in Him (John 17:1-26).

So that's what it means to hallow His name, but how do we do that? How can we know the prayer is answered and that God's name has really been hallowed? We are asking God to let His name be hallowed, and the implication is that that will be effected through us. "Let Your name be hallowed in our lives."

But how? How do we really reverence God?

Number one, we hallow His name when we believe He exists. Hebrews 11:6 says, "He that cometh to God must believe that he is." That is where it begins, and the Scripture never tries to prove God's existence. Why? Because God is self-evident.

Astronomer Sir James Jeans said, "No astronomer could ever be an atheist."

Immanuel Kant, the philosopher, had this right, at least: "The law within us and the starry heavens above us drive us to God."

But it does not stop there. You can believe God

exists and still not hallow His name.

Second, we must know the kind of God He is. Many people say they believe in God, but they don't hallow His name because they don't believe in the God He really is. Swearing is not the only way you can take the name of the Lord in vain. You take the name of the Lord in vain every time you think a thought about God that is not true. When you doubt God, when you disbelieve Him, when you question Him, you are taking His name in vain.

The Greeks had gods that were far afield from the true God. They had invented gods who fought wars, had quarrels, had lovers, felt hatred, seduced each other, and committed adulteries, immoralities, perversions, and atrocities. When men invent gods, their gods turn out like them.

So to tell the Greeks to hallow and exalt and reverence their gods would be ridiculous. Their gods were as vile as they were.

Some have tried to say that the true God is cruel, savage, vindictive, and harsh because He punished certain nations. Even Job fell into that sin in Job 30:21 when he said, "Thou art become cruel to me."

God is accused of being unloving, of indiscriminately banishing people to an eternal hell, a national ally of Israel who goes around slaughtering other people. When you think wrong thoughts like that about God, you don't understand who He really is, and you have not hallowed His name.

Third, we hallow His name when we are *constantly* aware of His presence. We need to live every day of our lives giving place to God. In Psalm 16:8, David wrote, "I have set the LORD always before me." That's the key.

How about you? To reverence God is to live in

His consciousness. Most of our thoughts of God are spasmodic; sometimes intense, sometimes absent. But to really hallow His name is to draw conscious thoughts of God into every daily thought, word, and action.

To hallow God, then, means that we must believe that He exists, that He is who He says He is, and that we must be constantly aware of His presence. But you could do all three of those things and still not reverence God or hallow His name.

Fourth, we hallow God's name when we live a life of obedience to Him. To do all the rest and to then disobey cuts off the capability to reverence His name. The request is not just that God's name be hallowed in heaven; it's not just that God's name be hallowed around the world; it's that God's name be hallowed in me, that I may be a vehicle for His holiness.

Martin Luther asked, "How is God's name hallowed amongst us?" His answer was, "When both our doctrines and our living are truly Christian."

That's where prayer begins. Before we start asking for what we want, we need to ask for what we should be. When you have the right thoughts of God and you do the right deeds from God, you are hallowing His name. The first part of the Disciples' Prayer is really saying, "God, teach me the truth and help me live it."

First Corinthians 10:31 says to do "all to the glory of God." The Bible says we glorify and obey God by confessing Him as Lord, by confessing sin, by faith, by bearing fruit, by praising Him, by being content, by proclaiming His truth, by evangelizing, by sexual purity, by spiritual unity.

Gregory of Nyssa prayed this: "May I become through Thy help blameless, just and holy. May I abstain from every evil, speak the truth and do justly. May I walk in the straight paths shining with temperance, adorned with incorruption, beautiful through wisdom and prudence. May I meditate upon the things that are above and despise what is earthly, for a man can glorify God in no other way save by his virtue, which bears witness that the divine power is the cause of his goodness."

Hallowed be the name of God.

4

"Thy Kingdom Come"—
The Program of Prayer

"Thy kingdom come." An incredible statement—three simple words in both English and Greek, yet they open to us something so vast that one approaches this text like a little boy with a pail standing before the uncharted seas, wondering how to fit it all into his bucket.

There is no way one can contain it, no way one can articulate all that is here. But if I can just whet your appetite, you can spend the rest of your life examining all that is beyond this.

Frances Havergal has beautifully written in one of her hymns this verse to Jesus Christ:

> Oh, the joy to see Thee reigning,
> Thee, my own beloved Lord.
> Every tongue Thy name confessing,
> Worship, honor, glory, blessing,
> Brought to Thee with one accord.
> Thee, my Master and my Friend,
> Vindicated and enthroned,
> Unto earth's remotest end,
> Glorified, adored, and owned.

The one who has the right to rule and reign is

none other than the King Himself, the King of kings and Lord of lords, Jesus Christ.

When David wanted to build a temple for the Lord, God told him through the prophet Nathan that he could not because he "was a man of blood." But though God kept from him one great joy, in return He gave him one great promise in 2 Samuel 7:12. In effect, God said, "Though you will not build My house, through your loins will come a child, and of that child shall be built a kingdom which shall never end."

And so the promise of the kingdom to the King, the eternal Son, is given. Throughout the Old Testament runs the promise of a coming King, One upon whose shoulders would be the government, says Isaiah, One who would have sway in the earth. A Savior, a Monarch, a King, a Messiah.

The very word *Messiah* means "anointed one." God's program centers on a person. It is not a plan without a person. Such is the hope of Israel, the hope of the church, the hope of the world.

Jesus Christ the King will consummate history. In Daniel we see the image smashed by a flying stone, representative of Christ, and the stone fills the whole earth. The symbolism is clear—Christ crushes the kingdoms of men and establishes His own.

Christ is inseparable from His kingdom. To pray, "Thy kingdom come," means nothing more or less than, "Christ reign, here and now." A true child of God concerns himself not with his own plans and desires, but with the determinate program of God, revealed in the person of Jesus Christ.

Praying right does not mean letting God in on our plans, but calling for God to fulfill His own. Too often our prayers are filled with our kingdoms, our plans, our rules, our reign, our causes.

Have you noticed yourself rushing into God's presence to unload your needs on Him? We have a bent toward self that is no better illustrated than in a newborn baby, who knows nothing of letting someone else have a choice.

A screaming baby is unable to deal with a mother who says, "I'm about to get around to you." The baby understands only one thing, and it's me, me, me.

We grow up, but we don't change much, do we? Advertising moguls begin when we are in junior high and high school to tell us we are the kings of our own castles, that we are to determine our own destinies, govern our own lives.

But when God invades a life, all of a sudden the command of the Word is *Thy* name by hallowed, *Thy* kingdom come, and *Thy* will be done. That goes against the grain. When you sincerely believe and genuinely confess Christ as Lord and King of your life, you are saying that the direction of your life is aimed at the exaltation of the Lord Jesus Christ.

Your own causes are valid only insofar as they are in accord with the eternal causes of God, revealed in Christ. When I pray, "Thy kingdom come," I am saying to God's Holy Spirit, "Spirit of Christ within me, take control and do what You will for Your glory."

Oh, that we could be preoccupied with the things of God, that we could be lost in His kingdom. Then we would value things that should be valued, and no man could ever take anything away from us.

People often ask me, What is going to happen to America? They say, Aren't you concerned about

America? Well, I am, in the sense that this is my homeland and I'm grateful to God for putting me here. I'm thankful for the freedoms here, but frankly, my concern is God's kingdom.

America will go the way of all the rest of the nations. Inexorably built into America is the inevitable hour indicated by God's Word: "Righteousness exalteth a nation, but sin is a reproach to any people" (Proverbs 14:34).

No nation will last, because built into all are the sinful seeds of their own damnation. We have already abandoned God's causes, our biblical standards, our morality. We are on the way back down. We know that, but America is not the issue. The issue is the kingdom of Christ and His causes, and no one can ever touch the things that really matter.

If America's eventual conquerors ever come after me and take everything I have and put me in jail, they can never touch what is really valuable to me. They can take my car and my house, my clothes, a few trinkets, all that stuff; but they cannot take the love I have for my wife or her love for me. They can't take the love I have for my children or their love for me. They can't take the love I have for God's people or their love for me. They can never touch my friendships.

But most of all, they can never touch Christ in my life, and they can never touch anything in His kingdom.

And so I invest my life there. My causes become God's causes.

The kingdom will go on, and the gates of hell will never prevail against it. Because America is not the ultimate issue does not mean that we are not to pray for our leaders; we are, the Bible tells us. But we are to pray that they act and think in accord with God's principles.

God's program is to exalt Christ. The consummation of history will be in the reign and rule of Christ. The Talmud says, "That prayer in which there is no mention of the Kingdom of God is no prayer at all."

The kingdom is the heart of the matter. Before we go bursting into His presence with all our petitions, we need to stop long enough to consider His causes and His kingdom, and affirm our yearning that He be glorified in His purposes.

Why is that so hard?

As soon as we desire to live a holy life for Him, we run right into the kingdom that exists in this world, which the Bible says is the kingdom of darkness. Satan challenges the effort of a believer to live a hallowed life. Therefore, subsequent to saying, "Hallowed by Thy name," we must say, "Thy kingdom come."

If Satan's kingdom is not withstood, there can be no hallowing of God's name. Unless we are, as Paul said, transformed from the kingdom of darkness into the kingdom of His dear Son (Colossians 1:13), we cannot hallow His name. Until Christ's rule is established, we have no capacity to hallow His name.

His kingdom cannot ever come until His will is done, because His kingdom and His will are inseparable.

Let's look more closely at the phrase "Thy kingdom come."

The word "kingdom," *basileia* in the Greek, means "rule" or "reign." I wish that everywhere that word appears in Scripture it had been translated "reign." I think that says something that "kingdom" does not.

"Kingdom" makes us think of land and of people

riding horses, pomp and ceremony, maidens and
knights, and castles and moats and walls and laws
and all that. Even Pilate asked Jesus if He was a
king, implying, "What kind of a king are you?"
(John 18:33-37).

Jesus replied, "My kingdom is not of this world"
(v. 36).

His kingdom is the rule and reign of Christ, His
sovereignty, for which we are to pray.

These three words "Thy kingdom come" introduce three questions.

Number one, whose is the kingdom? It's "thy"
kingdom. Who is "thy?"

Matthew 6:9 says it's *God's* kingdom, not a
human kingdom. We are not of this world. We have
been translated out of this world; our citizenship is
not here. We are sojourners and pilgrims. We look
for a city whose builder and maker is God.

I'm amazed how people think they can preserve
the church through politics. It cannot be done. No
human institution can dovetail with the kingdom,
and that is why when Christians endeavor to advance the kingdom through politics, they find
themselves with strange bedfellows.

One of the tragedies in the early years of America
was that the church relinquished to the government the care of widows and orphans. Now the
government has taken over social responsibilities
that belong to the church, and we don't know how
to get them back again. If somebody had thought
long ago that the kingdom cannot be run through
the government, maybe we would not have gotten
into this.

But "thy kingdom" is unique. Man-made kingdoms come and go. Egypt came and went, Syria
came and went, Assyria came and went, Babylon

came and went, Alexander the Great conquered everything from Europe to India and the north of Europe into Egypt. But it too is gone; nothing is left of that great empire. Historians tell us that at least twenty-one great civilizations are extinct.

What Daniel said in reference to Babylon could refer to all nations of the world: "God hath numbered thy kingdom, and finished it. . . . Thou art weighed in the balances, and art found wanting. . . . Thy kingdom is divided" (Daniel 5:26-28). Earthly kingdoms go the way of all flesh—the descending power of sin, decay, distress, and destruction are inevitable.

But the kingdom of God is bigger than any nation. Our Lord said to seek first the kingdom of God and His righteousness, and He would take care of all those other things that earthly kingdoms provide for physical well-being (Matthew 6:33).

And so what are our prayers? "Lord, I pray that You will do whatever advances Your kingdom, whatever brings Your rule and Your reign."

Whose is the kingdom? His.

Second, what is the kingdom? What is the rule and reign of Christ? The kingdom of heaven, or the kingdom of God (Matthew 19:23-24 uses both to refer to the same reality), is a phrase used by Jesus more than any other. He said this in Luke 4:43: "I must preach the kingdom of God . . . for therefore am I sent."

Whatever this kingdom is, it is the heart of His message. It is the heart of the plan, the heart of history, the apex of humanity. Nothing else matters.

Jesus spent all of His time with His disciples teaching them the kingdom, the kingdom, the kingdom. And when He died and rose again, He had forty more days. Acts 1:2-3 says He appeared to His disciples and gave them commandments pertaining to the kingdom of God.

Jesus spoke of the kingdom in three ways: past, present, and future. He spoke in Matthew 8:11 of the kingdom past that embodied Abraham, Isaac, and Jacob. He spoke of the kingdom present in Luke 17:21; "the kingdom of God is within you." And He spoke of the future when He prayed, "Thy kingdom come."

What is this kingdom that is past, present, and future all at the same time? In John 18:36 Jesus said, "My kingdom is not of this world," so whatever it is, it will not be like what we are used to. Christ's kingdom is both universal and earthly.

God is the universal King, and He mediates that rulership through His Son, by whom He made the worlds, and of whom is said in Colossians 1:17, "He is before all things, and by him all things consist." That is the universal kingdom. It is established in heaven, and the Disciples' Prayer is to let it come to this earth. This one little infinitesimal speck of sand in an infinite universe that rebels against holy God, let it be brought into harmony with His will.

It's a great concept. Although His name is hallowed in heaven, it is not always so on earth. The purpose of prayer, then, is to bring His kingdom to earth in all aspects that He might put down sin, rebellion, and evil.

There is coming a day when He will rule and reign, when our prayers will fully be answered.

Third, how does it come? What features lead to the consummation of His rule on earth?

Number one, conversion. He brings His rule to this earth when He reigns in lives. Christ *is* His kingdom, and you will never separate Him from it. He mediates it through the believer. That's why the Bible says we are priests and kings.

To pray, "Thy kingdom come," is to pray that He may take up His reigning residence in the hearts and lives of those who are in rebellion. It is a prayer for salvation, for kingdom citizenship.

The kingdom of God includes then an invitation that involves repentance. Jesus said, "Repent: for the kingdom of heaven is at hand." Mark 1:14-15 sums it up so well: "Jesus came into Galilee, preaching the gospel of the kingdom."

Kingdom citizenship is granted when one repents and believes.

That demands an act of the will. Jesus once told a scribe, "Thou art not far from the kingdom" (Mark 12:34).

He meant, "You've got the head knowledge, you just haven't made the choice yet." You can know about it and make some effort toward it, but until you make that final decision commitment, you do not enter the kingdom, and the rule of Christ is not established in your heart.

The kingdom, then, has an internal aspect. Such an internal kingdom, offered by an invitation that demands repentance and a choice to turn away from sin and toward God, is available to every man. That is conversion.

How should you respond? Jesus said, "Seek ye first the kingdom of God, and His righteousness" (Matthew 6:33). You should be seeking it.

Luke 16:16 says, "The law and the prophets were [proclaimed] until John [the Baptist]: since that time the kingdom of God is preached, and every man presseth [is forcing his way] into it."

There are a lot of ways to interpret that, but I like

the one that takes the verb *biazomai*—which really means "to enter violently"—so that when people whose hearts are right see the kingdom, they rush into it and literally seize it violently.

We ought to pray, "Thy kingdom come," in the sense that men be converted, rushing to grasp the reign of Christ in their lives.

And we ought to value it. Matthew 13 quotes Jesus: "The kingdom of heaven is like unto a treasure" (v. 44) and a "pearl of great price" (v. 46).

I believe the kingdom also comes by commitment. If you are a Christian, He is Lord and He is ruling, but there is in the Christian life a time daily for us to affirm that we bow the knee to that lordship. That's commitment. I call it responding to the royalty residing in us.

That is what Paul meant in Romans 14:17, writing to Christians: "The kingdom of God is not meat and drink; but righteousness, and peace, and joy in the Holy Ghost."

As I give myself over to the virtues the Spirit wants to produce in my life, I am asking that the fullness of Christ's reign be made manifest in me. In that sense, His kingdom comes.

Some people have taken those first two ways the kingdom comes—conversion and commitment—and assumed that that's all there is. I cannot accept that. There is one more way the kingdom comes.

The kingdom comes in consummation. One day the heavens will split open, and Jesus Christ will descend and plant His feet on the Mount of Olives, and He will establish His kingdom in this world.

Paul paints a beautiful portrait of Christ's coming to receive His kingdom in 1 Thessalonians 4:17. The saints rise in the air "to meet the Lord." In the extrabiblical literature, the Greek word *apantesis* portrayed citizens leaving their city to greet visiting royalty. Then they accompanied their royal visitor back to the city and honored him.

At the rapture, Christ will come to meet His redeemed citizens and to call them out of the earthly kingdom in preparation for His soon-coming rule. They will come into His presence, but instead of immediately returning, they will wait seven years while Christ conquers the remaining enemies in His earthly domain (Revelation 6-19).

At His second coming, He will complete the victory and return with His redeemed citizens to consummate the kingdom. The saints of heaven and the redeemed remnant of earth will then rule and reign with the Lord God Almighty as His priests for a thousand years (Revelation 1:6; 20:6).

Revelation tells us it will be a thousand-year kingdom, in which He will set things right and rule with a rod of iron, and the world will finally hear the answer to the Lord's prayer that the universal kingdom become the earthly kingdom.

The world will see Jesus Christ reigning here, when the curse is reversed and this earth is like God meant it to be before the Fall.

Jesus is coming again.

He will rule on the earth on the throne of David in the city of Jerusalem and will set right the curses that have been brought to this earth. Like Peter, I look to and hasten the day when He comes. I hear John saying again and again, "Jesus is coming, Jesus is coming, Jesus is coming." Finally, he says, in Revelation 22:20, "Even so, come, Lord Jesus."

We might ask the question, How does one become qualified to pray, "Thy kingdom come"? The answer is, By changing citizenship. And how does one change citizenship? By conversion. And how

does one live out that citizenship? By commitment.
And how is that citizenship fully realized? By consummation.

That glorious day is coming, and in the meantime
the kingdom is in your midst as He reigns and rules
in the hearts of His people.

5

"Thy Will Be Done"—
The Plan of Prayer, Part 1

Prayer works.

Abraham's servant prayed, and Rebekah appeared.

Jacob wrestled and prayed and prevailed with the angel, and Esau's mind was turned from twenty years of revenge.

Moses prayed, and Amalek was struck.

Joshua prayed, and Achan was discovered.

Hannah prayed, and Samuel was born.

David prayed, and Ahithophel hanged himself.

Asa prayed, and victory was won.

Jehoshaphat prayed, and God turned away his enemies.

Isaiah and Hezekiah prayed, and in twelve hours 185,000 Assyrians were slain.

Daniel prayed, and the lions were muzzled.

Mordecai and Esther prayed, and the plot to destroy the Jews was thwarted and Haman was hanged on his own gallows.

Nehemiah prayed, and the king's heart was softened in a moment.

Elijah prayed, and there were three years of drought. He prayed again, and it rained.

Elisha prayed, and a child was raised from the dead.

Believers prayed, and Peter was released from jail.

But beyond all that, there is the explicit statement of the Word of God itself that prayer is effective. James 5:16 says, "The effectual fervent prayer of a righteous man availeth much."

If God answered Elijah's prayer, God will answer our prayers. Elijah may have been a prophet, but he was also a mere man as we are (James 5:17).

Jesus said we are to pray always and not to faint (Luke 18:1). Paul said we are to pray without ceasing and with all prayer and supplication; (Ephesians 6:18; 1 Thessalonians 5:17).

The thought we are concentrating on in the next two chapters is "Thy will be done in earth, as it is in heaven." In just saying those words, we are immediately faced with a dilemma. Do we really need to say, "God, Your will be done"?

Isn't God sovereign anyway? Some people have taken this concept so far that they question the validity of prayer altogether. The question inevitably comes up, Isn't God in charge of everything? And if He is, and it's all working according to His plan, then why are we praying, "Thy will be done"?

The question then arises, Does God change His mind? Are we really praying to get God to do something other than what He had planned?

Someone else may ask, Does our will prevail over God's will? Does He have to answer our prayers at all? Just how does prayer fit into who God is?

If prayer is effective, than how can God still be absolutely sovereign?

I don't know. It is one of the great paradoxes of Scripture that tells me again that God's mind is infinitely beyond my own. This is an impossible dilemma for me and for everyone else. But it is no contradiction at all to our majestic God.

It is akin to the question, Who wrote the book of Matthew—Matthew or the Holy Spirit? Is either answer wrong? Are both right?

Who lives the Christian life? You say, not I but Christ in me. Yet Paul says, "I beat my body to bring it into subjection." Who is doing it? You or He? Both? Yes.

Another paradox: Was Jesus God or man? It's like asking, Is it colder in the mountains or in winter? Jesus is God, and He is man. He cannot be 200 percent of Himself in the limits of our comprehension, but somehow in the infinite mind of God, those seeming paradoxes exist.

We could go on forever with mind-bogglers, but my point is that when you find paradoxes in Scripture—and you'll find them at all the points of great doctrine—do not come up with some compromise and ruin both sides.

That's the temptation, but let them both exist. If God allows them, surely we can too. We don't have to fully understand. If we could understand the mind of God, what would that make us? God *is* sovereign. God *has* predetermined the flow of the universe. God *does* know the end from the beginning. God *will* do what God will do. And some day we will know as we are known.

On the other hand, prayer *does* work, and if you don't understand how those fit together, don't let your theology destroy your prayer life!

Once you have decided that you can accept the fact that prayer—even to the predeterminate God—is valid and vital, a right attitude toward prayer is achieved.

The entire Disciples' Prayer must be something that flows out of a truly committed heart. It ought to be a definition of your spirit, your attitude toward God, what is inside you. An unknown author put it this way:

I cannot say "our" if I live only for myself.

I cannot say "Father" if I do not endeavor each day to act like His child.

I cannot say "who art in heaven" if I am laying up no treasure there.

I cannot say "hallowed be Thy name" if I am not striving for holiness.

I cannot say "Thy kingdom come" if I am not doing all in my power to hasten that wonderful event.

I cannot say "Thy will be done" if I am disobedient to His Word.

I cannot say "in earth as it is in heaven" if I'll not serve Him here and now.

I cannot say "give us this day our daily bread" if I am dishonest or seeking things by subterfuge.

I cannot say "forgive us our debts" if I harbor a grudge against anyone.

I cannot say "lead us not into temptation" if I deliberately place myself in its path.

I cannot say "deliver us from evil" if I do not put on the whole armor of God.

I cannot say "Thine is the kingdom" if I do not give the King the loyalty due Him from a faithful subject.

I cannot attribute to Him the power if I fear what men may do.

I cannot ascribe to Him the glory if I'm seeking honor only for myself, and I cannot say "forever" if the horizon of my life is bounded completely by time.

In our study of the entire prayer, we have come to this great thought of God's plan: "Thy will be done."

Whenever we pray, we are to pray in accord with God's will. The literal Greek of this simple statement says something like this, "Your will, whatever You wish to happen, let it happen," and then the Greek adds, "As in heaven, so in earth."

In other words, "God, do what you want." That is the bottom line in prayer.

David prayed that way in Psalm 40:8 when he said, "I delight to do thy will, O my God."

We see it in Christ, don't we? John 4:34, "My meat is to do the will of him that sent me." John 6:38, "For I came down from heaven, not to do mine own will, but the will of him that sent me." Matthew 12:50, "Whosoever shall do the will of my Father . . . the same is my brother, and sister, and mother."

There are people who pray, "Thy will be done," in an attitude of resentment. They believe they cannot escape the inevitable, and they're angry about it. This reflects a lack of knowledge about God. They imagine Him to be oppressive, dictatorial, overbearing, selfish, and cruel.

You may have prayed, "Thy will be done," almost through clenched teeth. Maybe after the loss of a precious child, a broken love, or some other tragedy.

Omar Khayyam had an amazing view of God as a checker player with total power, moving the pieces of our lives at His whim and then putting them back into the closet.

Other people say, "Thy will be done," not necessarily out of resentment but out of what I call passive resignation. That is not so much a lack of knowledge about God, but a lack of faith in His good intention for their lives. What they are really saying is, "God, I don't have any kind of faith that my prayer is going to do a bit of good, but I'm going to say this phrase to cover everything just in case."

Julian was the Roman who followed Constantine as emperor. Constantine had made the Roman Empire Christian, at least in name. The people talked about Christ, and Christianity was the religion of the state. But along came Julian the Apostate who wanted to scuttle Christianity and take the whole empire back to the worship of the pagan deities.

He was unsuccessful and eventually mortally wounded in battle. Historians tell us that as he was bleeding to death, he scooped up a handful of his own blood, tossed it in the air and said, "You have conquered, O Man of Galilee." I don't know that he was even bitter, but he *was* resigned to the inevitable.

Is that how you pray? Is "Thy will be done" just something you tack on to cover the inevitable because you don't really believe your prayer is going to make a difference anyway?

A classic illustration of this is found in Acts 12 when the church was praying for the imprisoned Peter. At the house of Mary, the mother of John Mark, they prayed, "Oh, God, release Peter. Oh, Lord, free Peter."

Meanwhile, the angel of the Lord delivered Peter from jail. Peter thought he ought to go across town to the prayer meeting and see the folks, but when he arrived they didn't even believe the maid when she said he was at the door. They said, "Oh, Rhoda, don't you know he's in prison? That's why we're praying here. Now get back on your knees."

But she persisted, and when they finally brought Peter in, the Bible says they were all astonished. Why? Because they were like so many other evangelicals who fall into that passive resignation that makes our prayers insipid.

To say, "Thy will be done in earth," assumes that it is not always done, and that is true of some other elements of this prayer.

We say, "Hallowed be thy name," but there are times and places when His name is not hallowed.

We say, "Thy kingdom come," yet there are hearts that reject His reign.

So when we say, "Thy will be done in earth, as it is in heaven," we have to admit that not everything that happens in the world is His will. Otherwise, the petition is pointless, and the Lord is asking us to mumble meaningless things.

Very often you hear of someone telling the parents of a child who has died, "It's the Lord's will."

Or a mother, who is so needed by her husband and children, becomes wracked with cancer and is fading fast, and somebody says, "It's the Lord's will."

Or you hear about a flood or an earthquake or a fire or a train wreck or an airplane crash or a famine or starving boat people, and you say, "It's the Lord's will."

You know what? If you start looking at things that way, it will suck the energy right out of your prayer life. Would you want to pray to the person who wills such horrible catastrophes? I wouldn't.

Those things are *not* God's will. Those are the kinds of things that Jesus came into the world to stop. His will must be seen as His preferred purposes for those He loves. God "is not willing that any should perish" (2 Peter 3:9), but people are perishing all over.

God's will is that men be saved and come to the knowledge of the truth, but not all men do. God's will is done in heaven, but it is not always done on earth. You say, well God *allows* those things. That's right. But do not make the mistake of calling them the expressions of His will.

It is not God's will that people die, otherwise why would He come to destroy death?

It is not God's desire that people go to hell, or why would He die and provide the salvation that keeps them from going there? He made hell for the devil and his angels (Matthew 25:41).

I'm confident that God allowed man the choice to do good or evil. I believe man has a choice; I also believe God is sovereign, and that's another of those paradoxes I have to accept. God *has* allowed sin; He *has* allowed the cup of iniquity to be full. But it is *not* the expression of His will.

God is not responsible for sin, and He is not responsible for its consequences. Matthew 10:28 says, "Fear not them which kill the body . . . but rather fear him which is able to destroy both soul and body in hell." That refers to God. God will destroy soul and body in hell. It cannot refer to Satan, because he is one who will himself be destroyed eventually.

Yet 2 Peter 3:9 says that God is not willing that any should perish. God's holiness, justice, and righteousness must provide for dealing with sin, but death is *not* God's will. He wept over the city of Jerusalem and said, "Thou that killest the prophets, and stonest them which are sent unto thee, how often would I have gathered thy children, even as a hen gathereth her chickens under her wings, and ye would not!" (Matthew 23:37).

God so loved the world that he gave his Son.

Why? That men might be saved from judgment.

Why then did God allow sin?

That is a question theologians have discussed for a long time. Lucifer fell. How did that happen? Did pride come from inside him? No, he was perfect. Did it come from outside him? No, the environment was perfect. Where did it come from? I don't know.

God knows. Lucifer sinned.

Then God had two options: to destroy Lucifer immediately or to allow evil to run its full course. I believe God chose the latter rather than have the constant possibility of another rebellion. He let the uprising go full blast, and it will ultimately run itself out, like a comet that fades, forever dead and never to rise again.

All eternity will be saved from another sinful expression. God let it run. He let it gather all the host of angels who wanted it. He let it gather the hearts of willing men, all the while providing a way of escape for every man who would come to him. He has allowed evil to run its full course, because He sees the bigger picture of all eternity, but during this time when evil is running the gamut, it is not by any stretch of the imagination the will of God.

It fits within His tolerance only in order that it may be destroyed. So you cannot say everything is God's will. Such a statement is simplistic.

There are also some who pray, "Thy will be done," with theological reservations. To them it's theology, simply God's doing what He's doing because He runs everything and it's all cut and dried. No pleading, no intensity, no passion. I can't honestly say I ever met anybody who really took this hard line who had much of a prayer life.

I wonder if that attitude can ever bring about a

heart like David's, who said, "O how I love thy law!" (Psalm 119:97).

When we say, "Thy will be done," we are not factually affirming theology with indifference. We have a responsibility to be personally involved.

In Luke 18, Jesus was trying to teach that men ought always to pray and not to faint. In other words, you don't want to just stop praying—you don't want to become weary, lose heart, or become indifferent. And then He tells a story:

"There was in a city a judge, which feared not God, neither regarded man. And there was a widow in the city; and she came unto him, saying, Avenge me of mine adversary."

She had been wronged, and she wanted the king to mete out justice. He would not do it for a while, "but afterward he said within himself, Though I fear not God, nor regard man; yet because this widow troubleth me, I will avenge her, lest by her continual coming she weary me."

He was so sick of hearing the woman; he was going to do what she asked just to get rid of her. If an unjust judge will give justice to a badgering woman, what will a just, loving, righteous, caring Father God give to His children?

The parallel Jesus drew was obviously not between God and the judge, because there is no parallel at all, but between the widow and the petitioner. The woman refused to accept an unjust situation, and she persisted with her case.

That is a good word for us. We have a right to refuse to accept certain situations in the world. We have a right to refuse to accept the way things are, and to pray persistently that God would do them the way they ought to be done.

I believe praying in this way is an act of rebellion

against the world in its fallenness. It is rebellion against accepting as normal what is pervasively abnormal. It is rebellion against the usurper and against every agenda and scheme and interpretation and deed and word and movement at odds with the will of God.

We literally have to assault the gates of heaven. We will not stand by and let our theology and our passive resignation or our resentment assign it all to God's will.

It is not God's preference. We must pray, "Thy will be done in earth," because it is not being done on earth.

Jesus never accepted the status quo. He didn't say, "Oh, well, the cross, it's Your will." He said, in effect, "Father, does it have to be this way? I rebel against this sinfulness. I rebel against the power of sin to take My life. I rebel against the necessity for bearing sin. I rebel against these things that violate the sanctity of Your holy universe."

He was in the midst of His rebellion against the fallenness of the world, and the disciples were sleeping.

How about your prayer life? Are you praying, "Thy will be done in earth," because you feel you have no choice? Are you indifferent due to your theology?

There are better reasons to pray, "Thy will be done."

6

"In Earth, as It Is in Heaven"—The Plan of Prayer, Part 2

All the elements of the Disciples' Prayer focus on God. Even the petitions that relate to us really depend upon Him. It is He who must give our daily bread, He who must forgive our trespasses, and He alone who can lead us not into temptation.

The prayer is primarily an act of worship, an engagement in the process of sanctification.

Prayer is designed not to change God, but to change us.

Have you ever wondered how the angels do God's will? To know how it is to be done on earth, we need to know how it is done in heaven. Eight words summarize all that Scripture teaches regarding the way the angels do the will of God.

First, unwaveringly. There's never a discussion. On earth the Lord prods and pokes, and maybe we get moving sooner or later, but in heaven there's an unwavering commitment to His will.

Second, completely. There are no alternatives, no gaps, no omissions.

Third, sincerely. They are eager, waiting for the next command so they can hurry to accomplish it.

Fourth, willingly. Do you know how many wills there are in heaven? One. There were two once, but one got kicked out.

Fifth, fervently. They are aggressive in doing God's will.

Sixth, readily.

Seventh, swiftly.

And eighth, constantly.

It is summed up in Psalm 103:20: "Ye his angels . . . that do his commandments."

"Thy will be done in earth, as it is in heaven," means that on earth it should be done without wavering, completely, sincerely, willingly, fervently, readily, swiftly, and constantly.

That's well and good, you say, but what does it mean? It means that death of self is the beginning of a true prayer life. True prayer is dominated by His name, His kingdom, and His will, not ours. And thus David said, "I delight to do thy will, O my God." And thus Jesus said, "My meat is to do the will of him that sent me."

His name, His kingdom, His will—on earth as in heaven. In heaven His name is hallowed, His kingdom is come, He rules supreme, and His will is done, and so should it be here.

When we say, "Thy will be done," we are rebelling against the world in its fallenness. We are saying. "Your will is not being done in this world; Satan has too much power here. Your will is not being done in the hearts of men—they are turning their backs on You. Your will is not being done in my life and the lives of other believers living in disobedience."

God does not accept the world the way it is, or He

would not be busy changing it. He would not have come into the world to destroy death if He wanted to tolerate it. He wouldn't promise to wipe away every tear if He wanted to tolerate sorrow.

"Thy will be done" does not accept what is. Jesus did not come into the Temple in John 2 at the beginning of His ministry and say, "Well, look what's going on. It must be the will of God."

No. Everything in Him rebelled. He was furious with a righteous wrath. He made a whip, He flipped over tables, He chased people out, He lashed at people. The Bible tells us that the second time Jesus drove the money changers from the Temple, He was so furious that everybody ran and nobody took a penny with him (Mark 11:15-16).

Jesus knew the end from the beginning and yet never accepted the status quo. He fought it, He never resigned to it. He sought God's will.

Our problem in seeking His will is that we want our way. We have a disease called comfort, and the symptoms are that we love it, we crave it. It causes us to perceive prayer as making a difference in our circumstances rather than making a difference in us.

Prayer is not to change circumstances so much as it is to change how we relate to them. We are drawn into conformity to His blessed person and then, no matter what our circumstances, they become different because of our changed attitudes.

And I do believe that God changes circumstances. I've prayed for people, and they've been saved. God not only chooses those to be saved, but also the methods—and sometimes our prayer is part of those methods.

Three distinct terms describing God's will help us understand what we mean in a positive sense when we pray, "Thy will be done."

God's comprehensive will. By this I mean the vastness of God's all-inclusive, purposeful, tolerating will. In this massive concept of His will of purpose is encompassed the allowing of sin to run its course, the consummation of the ages, the establishing of the kingdom, the eternal state, and everything from heaven to hell and in between.

Jeremiah 51:29 says, "For every purpose of the LORD shall be performed." There is no question that His plan of the ages is on track, no question that God is working out His ultimate purposes.

Isaiah 14:24-27 says, "The LORD of hosts hath sworn, saying, Surely as I have thought, so shall it come to pass; and as I have purposed, so shall it stand. . . . This is the purpose that is purposed upon the whole earth, and this is the hand that is stretched out upon all the nations. For the LORD of hosts hath purposed, and who shall disannul it?"

It is not God's preference for people to be ill, but it is within His purpose to allow illness to accomplish His own ends.

It is not God's preference that death enter the human stream, but people die within His comprehensive purpose for His own end and His own glory. We know that "all things work together for good to them that love God, to them who are the called according to his purpose" (Romans 8:28). Though God does not will evil, He takes the things that happen in history and in our lives and puts them together for good.

Ephesians 1:9 says, "Having made known unto us the mystery of his will, according to his good pleasure which he hath purposed in himself." Here he is talking about salvation, the incredible forgiveness and redemption in God's great encompassing purpose. Then he goes on to talk about Jew and Gentile being one:

"That in the dispensation of the fulness of times, he might gather together in one all things in Christ, both which are in heaven, and which are on earth . . . according to the purpose of him who worketh all things after the counsel of his own will" (vv. 10-11).

God's great purpose is for a redeemed people, for a unified church, a body of saints for eternity. So how should we pray?

In Revelation 22:7, Jesus says, "Behold, I come quickly."

In verse 12, He also says, "Behold, I come quickly."

In verse 20, He says, "Surely, I come quickly."

What is the apostle John's response in the final verse? "Even so, come, Lord Jesus."

How do we pray in accord with His will of purpose? By joyously getting involved in the anticipation of the accomplishment of His divine ends. That's a great way to pray: "Lord, I know someday You're going to call out Your church, and You're going to bring back Jesus Christ to take us to be with Him. May it be, Lord, may it be."

It's going to happen—it's inevitable. He thought it, He purposed it, it's in the plan.

Do you ever get tired of the anxiety of this world? Do you ever long for the day when you know the freedom of the sons of God, when you are like Christ, and you can dwell in eternal glory with Him? I do. And so sometimes I will pray, "Lord, I know You're going to do it, and I just want to let You know You've got my vote. Go ahead, do it. The sooner the better." That's praying according to God's comprehensive will.

God's compassionate will. Included in this are the things that God wills that don't always happen;

they are His desires, but men may reject them.

For example, Jesus desired that Jerusalem be saved. In Matthew 23:37 and in Luke 13:34 He said, "Jerusalem, Jerusalem, I want to gather you, but you won't!" And in John 5:40 He said, "Ye will not come to me that ye might have life."

You remember that Jesus wept, but do you know that in Jeremiah 13:17 God says that when He must judge sinners, "Mine eyes . . . run down with tears?"

Peter says He is not willing that any should perish, "but that all should come to repentance" (2 Peter 3:9).

That is the heart's desire of God, and yet many will say in that last day, "Lord, Lord," and He will respond, "Depart from me, I never knew you" (Matthew 7:22-23). He desires all to be saved, but not all will be. That's the mysterious paradox of an absolutely sovereign God's allowing man his own volition.

God's commanding will is related to the Christian. It is the ardent desire of the heart of God that we who are His children obey Him completely and immediately with willing hearts.

And so when I pray, "Thy will be done," I'm saying, "Oh, God, fulfill Your comprehensive will in the world. Bring it to consummation. Take every struggle and trial in my life, every pain and anxiety, every sorrow, every sickness, every death, and somehow reverse those results of sin and fit them into Your eternal plan by Your infinite mind."

I'm also saying, "O God, there are people in my life and around this globe who don't know You. I pray that somehow the gospel would penetrate their hearts." That is His compassionate will.

Third, I am praying, "Lord, about your will of

command, I pray that I personally might be obedient."

Remember the three ways to see the kingdom? Through conversion, when Christ comes to reign in a heart; through commitment, when a believer lives according to righteousness, peace, and joy in the Holy Spirit; and in His second coming, when the kingdom comes to earth. I see the same three things here.

His *comprehensive will* embraces the ultimate end, the coming again, and the setting up of an eternal kingdom.

His *compassionate will* embraces conversion.

And His *commanding will* embraces the idea of obedient commitment in my life.

As Peter said so well in Acts 5:29, "We ought to obey God rather than men."

David said it all in the magnificence of Psalm 119, where he stated things like this: "[O God], make me to understand the way of thy precepts. . . . I have chosen the way of truth: thy judgments have I laid before me. . . . I will run the way of thy commandments. . . . Teach me, O Lord, the way of thy statutes; and I shall keep it unto the end. . . . I will delight myself in thy commandments. . . . Thy statutes have been my songs. . . . I will never forget thy precepts: for with them thou hast quickened me. . . . O how love I thy law!"

You know it's hard to pray that way. It's hard to be preoccupied with God in our prayers, and there's one basic reason—the major sin of the human heart—pride.

There are at least four billion wills on earth, and still only one in heaven. Only one of those wills is righteous. Every other is corrupt, and that four billion does not even include all the fallen angelic hosts.

Only one will is done in heaven, and it needs to be done on earth. But pride always stands in the way.

How do we get pride out of the way? Romans 12:1-2 says, "I beseech you therefore, brethren, by the mercies of God, that you present your bodies a living sacrifice [self-denial, humility], holy, acceptable unto God, which is your reasonable service. And be not conformed to this world: but be ye transformed by the renewing of your mind, that ye may prove what is that good, and acceptable, and perfect *will of God*" (italics added).

Until we lay our lives on the altar, until we become living sacrifices, until our wills are dead, God's will cannot be manifest.

A living sacrifice is very different from what you might think. Abraham (in Genesis 22) strapped wood on Isaac's back, and all the way up Mount Moriah Abraham must have been saying, "This is very strange, God. You've told me to go up there and slay my son on the altar, and yet my son is the fulfillment of your covenant. You promised me a son when Sarah and I were so old, and now you tell me to lay him on the altar and kill him. This doesn't make sense."

But Abraham went all the way up there, strapped Isaac down, and was ready to plunge the knife into his heart. If he had done that, Isaac would have been a dead sacrifice, but Abraham would have been a living one. Abraham would have crucified all his own dreams, all his own hopes, all his own ambitions, all his own goals, all his own desires.

He literally would have died to himself, in obedience to God.

The question is not only, Can you die for Christ?

The question also is, Can you live selflessly for Him? If you will, you can know His good will. The one thing that always stands in the way of praying for God's will is our own will. When we learn to pray as we should, in conformity with His will, we change dramatically.

Prayer, then, is a sanctifying grace. It changes us. We do not pray to manipulate God. We do not pray to get God to do what we want. We don't pray with incantations and vain repetition to put on a show. We go into God's presence to hallow His name, bring His kingdom, and fulfill His will.

Summarily, prayer is a means of progressive sanctification, in which we learn to depend wholly upon God. The answers will come, but the dependency is the issue.

We are to pray, "Thy will be done on earth." The earth is us, right? Let me illustrate:

Author Philip Keller, visiting in Pakistan, read Jeremiah 18:2, "Arise, and go down to the potter's house, and there I will cause thee to hear my words." So he and a missionary went to the potter's house in that city.

In *A Layman Looks at the Lord's Prayer* [Chicago: Moody, 1976], pp. 90-96), he writes,

> In sincerity and earnestness, I asked the old master craftsman to show me every step in the creation of a masterpiece. . . . On his shelves were gleaming goblets and lovely vases and exquisite bowls of breathtaking beauty.
>
> Then, crooking a bony finger toward me, he led the way to a small, dark, closed shed at the back of his shop. When he opened its rickety door, a repulsive overpowering stench of decaying matter engulfed me. For a moment I stepped back from the edge of the gaping dark pit in the floor of the shed.
>
> "This is where the work begins," he said, kneel-

ing beside the black, nauseating hole. With his long thin arm he reached down into the darkness. His slim, skilled fingers felt around amid the lumpy clay searching for a fragment of material exactly suited to his task. "I add special kinds of grass to the mud," he remarked. "As it rots and decays, its organic content increases the colloidal quality of the clay. Then it sticks together better."

Finally his knowing hands brought up a lump of dark mud from the horrible pit where the clay had been tramped and mixed for hours by his hard, bony feet. With tremendous impact the first verses from Psalm 40 came to my heart . . . "He brought me up also out of an horrible pit, out of the miry clay." As carefully as the potter selected his clay, so God used special care in choosing me.

He walked, clay in hand, over to where a huge, round slab of stone stood in the center of his shop. . . . The great slab of granite, carved from the rough rock of the high Hindu Kush Mountains behind his home, whirled quietly . . . but what stood out most before my mind at this point was the fact that beside the potter's stool, on either side of him, stood two basins of water. Not once did he touch the clay . . . without first dipping his hands in the water . . .

The water was the medium through which the master craftsman's will and wishes were transmitted to the clay. His will actually was being done in earth . . . a most moving demonstration . . . that my Father's will and wishes are expressed and transmitted to me through the water of His own Word.

It is the water of the Word—the expressed will of God—that finds fulfillment in fashioning me to His will.

Suddenly, to Keller's astonishment, he saw the wheel stop. Gently the man picked out a piece of stone, and then later he stopped it again and picked out a larger piece. With the tenderness of his hand he could feel every rough spot, every stone, every small grain of sand. The two he had taken out were too large, and the would-be goblet was marred. So the potter crushed it in his hands.

In dismay I turned to my missionary friend and asked him in a hoarse whisper, "What will the potter do now?" The question was passed on. Looking up at me through eyes now clouded and sad, he replied with a sorrowful shrug of his tired old shoulders, "Just make a crude finger bowl from the same lump."

The word of God from Jeremiah came home to me like an arrow to its target: "So he [the potter—my God] made it again another vessel, as seemed good to the potter to make it" [Jeremiah 18:4].

The sobering, searching, searing question I had to ask myself in the humble surroundings of that simple potter's shed was this: Am I going to be a piece of fine china or just a finger bowl? Is my life going to be a gorgous goblet fit to hold the fine wine of God's very life from which others can drink and be refreshed? Or am I going to be just a crude finger bowl in which passersby will dabble their fingers briefly then pass on and forget all about it? It was one of the most solemn moments in all of my spiritual experiences.

"Father, Thy will be done in earth [in clay], in me, as it is done in heaven."

7

"Give Us This Day Our Daily Bread"—The Provision of Prayer, Part 1

Having focused on God (Thy name, Thy kingdom, Thy will), we turn now to the believer (give us, forgive us, lead us). Once God is given His rightful place, then we have the proper perspective toward ourselves.

The word *bread* opens to us the simplicity, the commonness of this petition, and yet suggests also a deep and profound meaning that demands our careful study.

Praying that God will give us this day our daily bread may at first seem irrelevant to us. I mean, when was the last time you prayed, "Lord, I plead with You to provide for me a meal"? I dare say your last mealtime prayer may have been more like, "Lord, please *prevent* me from eating another meal. Teach me self-discipline. I not only have enough bread for myself, but also for several others."

It does seem a little remote, doesn't it? You might think this prayer ought to be uttered by people in Bangladesh or Cambodia, but not in North America. But that only illustrates our lack of understanding of its marvelous truth.

By giving us our daily bread, forgiving us our debts, and by leading us, God hallows His name, brings His kingdom, and does His will on earth.

It is as if the second half of the Lord's Prayer brings God into human life. It's not that the first half butters Him up so we can really make request for what we want for our own sakes. No.

We are saying, "God, glorify Yourself in our daily provision. God, glorify Yourself in our constant forgiveness. God, glorify Yourself in the leading and the directing of your Holy Spirit in our lives. God, be on display in Your world, that Your kingdom may come to earth."

It is not a setting aside of God in any sense. We want God to be on display. If prayer becomes man-centered, it ceases to be the kind of prayer our Lord said should be characteristic of His kingdom.

In this prayer's three petitions that give God opportunity to glorify Himself, "Give us this day our daily bread" speaks of physical life. "And forgive us our debts, as we forgive our debtors" speaks of the mental life. And "Lead us not into temptation, but deliver us from evil" speaks of the spiritual life.

Bread is provision for the present, forgiveness takes care of the past, and leading takes care of the future.

Elton Trueblood writes, "In some congregations the gospel has been diminished to the mere art of self-fulfillment. Egocentricity is all that is left."

It is crucial that we remember that all those petitions in the Disciples' Prayer, though directed at our essential needs, are ways in which God's glory comes to earth and makes itself manifest.

J. I. Packer has said, "The prayer of a Christian is not an attempt to force God's hand, but it is a humble acknowledgment of helplessness and dependence."

So with the perspective that even this petition is for God's glory, let's look at "Give us this day our daily bread."

The word *bread* is really a broad term meaning all of man's physical needs, about which I want to make five points in this and the next chapter.

First, the *substance*. What is the substance here? It is bread, the physical provision. Man can't even be a spiritual being unless he is first a physical one. God has to begin with physical.

It thrills me to know that God, the God of celestial epochs, the God of space, the God beyond time, the God of eternity, the God who is infinitely holy and holds all the whirling worlds and the spinning stars in the palm of His hand—that same God cares that my physical needs are met. He even sets certain conditions for their being met, as we shall see in the next chapter.

Martin Luther, commenting on this petition, said, "Everything necessary for the preservation of this life is bread, including food, a healthy body, good weather, house, home, wife, children, good government, peace." He saw bread as all of the necessities, but not the luxuries, of life. What God chooses to give us by way of luxury is at His gracious hand. But He promises to give us the necessities.

Second, then, the *source* is a key consideration. God provides everything we need.

But you say, "John, in our lives we don't even have need."

Yes, we do. Although for us this is not the desperate cry of one who's starving, this petition is really an affirmation that all our substance comes from God. It is saying, "God, I realize You are the source of my life, my food, my shelter, my clothing."

It is similar to when I ask the Lord to forgive my sin and cleanse my life. Hasn't He already promised to do that? Yes, but He also says to keep confessing and recognizing His constant forgiveness.

I may not have to say, "O God, I don't have any food for my family; where is it going to come from?" But I will ever and always say, "God, everything I have and all that I share with those I love comes from Your good and gracious hand, and I trust You to continue to provide."

We tend to think that we provide everything for ourselves. We make our livings, we earn our wages, we buy our bread. What do we owe God? We're carrying our own loads. That's the way we think and operate.

When was the last time you said, "Lord, I thank You that I have food and clothes and shelter"? That's what God is after here. He cares about the little things. He is involved. He knows when a sparrow hops. He knows the number of hairs on your head.

We live in a day when people are afraid they are going to lose their existence because of the pollution of our resources. We're afraid of nuclear reactors messing up our environment. We're afraid of polluting our waters and of overpopulation. We're afraid of smog and air pollution. We're afraid of breaking up the ozone layer. We're afraid of poisoning our bodies with chemicals.

With all the money and all the resources we have, man is always on the brink of devastating his environment to the point where he has no resources. That ought to drive us to recognize that God upholds the whole thing.

There's going to come a day, says the book of Revelation, when God turns out the lights in the heavens, when He turns the rivers to blood, when He lets the whole world go crazy and the sea swallows up the ships and kills the fish, when devastation sweeps the world. The sun will go black and all the resources will be gone. The whole economic system will collapse, and it won't matter what you have. It won't be worth a nickel.

Scientists say that when all their calculations are done, there is an unknown element in the universe that makes it all hang together in constancy, and they don't even have a name for it. But I do. It's *God*.

Everything we have is from God. It is God who brings the rain to make things grow, it is He who cycles the seasons, it is He who produces the minerals in the soil to make the earth fertile, He who provides for us the animals from which we make our clothing and the petroleum from which we produce our synthetics.

In Genesis 1:29-31, God says, "Behold I have given you every herb bearing seed, which is upon the face of all the earth, and every tree, in the which is the fruit of a tree yielding seed; to you it shall be for meat [food]. And to every beast of the earth, and to every fowl of the air, and to every thing that creepeth upon the earth, wherein there is life, I have given every green herb for meat [food]: and it was so. And God saw every thing that he had made, and behold, it was very good."

God could have designed that we just eat mud. Mud for breakfast, mud for lunch, and mud for dinner all our lives, and that everything was colored gray. But He is a God of marvelous variety. Look around you. The tastes are myriad, the colors unending. And there is the same variety in everything.

First Timothy 4:3 says, "God hath created [these foods] to be received with thanksgiving of them which believe and know the truth." God has provided this incredible world of food for us, so we can express our thanks to Him. The rest of the world indulges without gratitude. Look at verse 4: "For every creature of God is good, and nothing to be refused, if it is received with thanksgiving; for it is sanctified by the word of God and prayer."

How are all these foods sanctified? By the word of God. Very clearly, God's Word says in Genesis 1:29-31 that it is all good. That sanctified it.

How else is it sanctified? By prayer. "When it is received with thanksgiving." The Word of God sanctifies it, and we sanctify it when we thank Him for it.

Do you really thank God for your food? You say, "Hey, we wouldn't have a meal without a prayer!" But do you just rattle it off to make sure the duty's done? Are you really thankful? Do you really see God as the source of everything?

Just think for a moment about what God has provided in the way of food. We have already stipulated that bread, or food, is not all that is covered by the word *bread* in this petition of the Lord's prayer, but consider only food for the moment.

God has provided plant food in grains like wheat, barley, millet, spelt, and corn.

According to Genesis 43:11 He provided nuts and vegetables like cucumbers, leeks, melons, onions, garlic, beans, lentils, bitter herbs, mint, dill, cumin, and—in Jeremiah 6:20—sweet cane.

Fruits are also a part of God's plant foods, such as grapes, raisins, olives, figs, pomegranates, apples, and then what Jeremiah and Amos call summer fruit.

There are animal foods, such as oxen, sheep, goats, pigs, lambs, and calves. In Deuteronomy 14:5 there is a list of seven animals that could be hunted for food, there are fish and even four types of insects as well, according to Leviticus 11.

There were also different kinds of fowl. In 1 Samuel 26, they ate partridge; in Exodus 16, they ate quail; in Leviticus 12, they ate pigeons; in Genesis 15, they ate turtledoves; and in Matthew, you find chickens.

There were also milk, curds or butter (in Genesis 18:8), cheese, eggs, and honey. The Lord provided an extensive array of condiments to flavor their food. Besides sugar from the sweet cane there were salt, mint, anise, all kinds of seeds, mustards, cumin, and any number of herbs.

It is thrilling to me that God has provided such an incredible abundance for us. When He told the children of Israel that they were going to a certain land, He said its characteristic was that it flowed with milk and honey. He meant it was a land of physical bounty. It is still true. Israel is one of the most fertile lands in all the world.

You have nothing, you eat nothing, you wear nothing that did not come from this earth, and every element in it is the work of the creative hand of God. It is the height of ingratitude to not recognize that and affirm that God is active daily in upholding His world so that it supports our physical needs.

God has even set up a network in order to have food for man. He has to feed the food that feeds man. The Bible says that for plant eaters there is herbage: for the ox there are grass and straw, for the horses there's barley, for the birds there are seeds, for the locusts there are plants, and God keeps the whole cycle going (see Psalm 104).

Rain is a gift from God. If it didn't fall, the grass and the plants would not grow, the animals would not eat, and we wouldn't eat either. We'd soon be dead.

You say, "Now wait a minute, I make my own way."

Just remember that it is God who gives you the power to get wealth. If you have the ability to bend your back, the ability to open your mouth and talk to make a living, the ability to think and make a living, it is God who gave you that facility.

And by the way, the money you got from the bank was made out of paper that came from trees, and the coins came from minerals. Talk about dependence! We are dependent on God.

First Chronicles 29:14 says, "All things come of thee, and of thine own have we given thee."

Next time you pray, remember that He is the source of all substance, and affirm that all your physical needs are met by God. Then ask Him humbly to continue to do it that His name may be glorified in your prayer of thanksgiving.

8

"Give Us This Day Our Daily Bread"—The Provision of Prayer, Part 2

In the Disciples' Prayer we ask nothing that does not hallow God's name, nothing that does not bring in His kingdom, and nothing that is not the expression of His will.

Having established that, we move from those elements specifically directed at God to those that relate to human need. We have already covered the first two of five features of this first human petition, "Give us this day our daily bread."

First was the *substance* requested, which is, of course, bread.

Second was the *source*, which is God, implied in the verb phrase "Give us." He is the one who desires to meet our physical need. And of course we know from James 1:17 that "every good gift and every perfect gift is from above, and cometh down from the Father of lights, with whom is no variableness, neither shadow of turning."

Third, then, what is the *supplication?* It is the verb *give.* That is the heart of the petition. What right do we have to ask God for this? Do I have some reason to say to God, "Give me my daily bread"? The only basis on which such a request would be valid is if God has promised to do that.

Psalm 37 sets in our minds a basic consideration that will be helpful in understanding how God desires to meet our physical needs. There are some conditions, and we will see those repeatedly.

God is not bound to meet everybody's physical needs. Psalm 37:3 says, "Trust in the LORD, and do good." That simple statement is profound because it encompasses the significance of salvation. Salvation is trusting God, which results in good works.

James says, "Faith without works is dead." If you are one who believes, then you have the promise that you will "dwell in the land, and verily thou shalt be *fed*" (Psalm 37:3, italics added).

Most of the promises in the Bible have to do with spiritual truth, but never to the exclusion of the physical. We would be of little spiritual good to the Lord if He didn't meet our physical need.

For the righteous there is promise; for the unrighteous there is judgment. Psalm 37:18-19 says, "The LORD knoweth the days of the upright: and their inheritance shall be for ever. And they shall not be ashamed in the evil time: and in the days of famine they shall be satisfied."

Though the unrighteous may perish, the righteous will have provision. In the same psalm, verses 25-27, David says, "I have been young, and now am old; yet have I not seen the righteous forsaken, nor his seed begging bread. He is ever merciful, and lendeth; and his seed is blessed. Depart from evil and do good."

There are many problems and struggles and famines in our world, but the issue is not really that the earth cannot provide food. Indira Ghandi herself said there is enough resource in India to feed that nation entirely and then export two-thirds of all that it produces.

Only fifteen percent of the harvestable land on the globe is being farmed, and only half of that every year. Our problem is not a lack of resources. Our problem is not too many people. By the early seventies a study revealed that there were less people per square mile in New York City— 42,000—than there had been fifty years earlier— 45,000 (Murray Norris, *The Myth of Overpopulation* [Clovis, Calif: Family Book Club, n.d.]).

The resources are there, but what cuts off those resources is a spiritual issue. If people were brought into the knowledge of God, God could provide for them. Psalm 33:18 says, "Behold, the eye of the Lord is upon those that fear him, upon them that hope in his mercy, to deliver their soul from death, and to keep them alive in famine."

Proverbs 3:5-6 says, "Trust in the LORD with all thine heart; and lean not unto thine own understanding. In all thy ways acknowledge him, and he shall direct thy paths." Verses 9-10: "Honour the LORD with thy substance, and with the firstfruits of all thine increase: So shall thy barns be filled with plenty, and thy presses shall burst out with new wine."

You say, "John, you're talking about Old Testament principles."

No, I'm not. Look at Matthew 7:7: "Ask, and it shall be given you; seek, and ye shall find; knock, and it shall be opened unto you." We usually equate that with spiritual things, in fact with coming to Christ and asking for salvation.

Then verse 8 says, "For everyone that asketh receiveth; and he that seeketh findeth; and to him that knocketh it shall be opened."

But just exactly what Christ is referring to is indicated in verses 9-11: "What man is there of you, whom if his son ask bread, will he give him a stone? Or if he ask a fish, will he give him a serpent? If ye then, being evil, know how to give good gifts unto your children, how much more shall your Father which is in heaven give good things to them that ask him?"

And that follows right on the heels of Matthew 6:25 and following, a marvelous text that says you do not need to worry about what you eat or what you drink or what you wear. You just "seek first the kingdom," and everything else will find its rightful place.

There have been times when the provision of food and shelter and clothing has been a super-natural act of God, but usually He meets the needs of His people through His other people. A child of God should have such a high view of the value of man that he seeks not only to meet his own needs, but also the needs of others.

James 2:16 says that if someone comes in naked and destitute, and you pat him on the back and say, "Brother, I hope the Lord meets your needs," it's questionable whether you are really regenerated. And in 1 John 3 it says that if a brother comes along and he has a great need, yet you close up the bowels of your compassion toward him, "how dwelleth the love of God in you?"

In parts of the world where there are no Christian roots, you see a low view of human life, great famine, and poverty. Nations that have known Christian teaching have a high respect for the value of man as created in God's image. There are isolated cases where that is not always true, but in general that is clearly the picture.

Take America, for example. Christianity gave this country a high view of life from the Bill of Rights on to meeting the needs of people in 1981. We're still concerned with the minimum wage, equality in education and work and opportunity, medical care, welfare, and all the rest. Where did we get that? Humanism never gave it to us. Humanists would obliterate that part of the population that is un-needed.

Abortionists would wipe out human beings. They aren't the ones who gave us a high view of man. America, in the midst of its practical atheism and humanism and immorality and departure from Christian truth still cannot shake the residual effect of a high view of man that came from the Word of God, even though many would never acknowledge that as the source of it.

Even the ungodly in our nation, as those in 1 Corinthians 7, are sanctified by the believers and receive the benefit. On the other hand, take India, the place where Hinduism was born and spawned the network of religions that enslaves the entire East. Hinduism is the source of Shintoism, Buddhism, Zoroastrianism, Confucianism, Taoism, and all the gurus and the mystics and the occultic Eastern religions.

But the entire legacy of Hinduism in the Orient is deprivation, because they do not believe that man is created in God's image. In the first place, they believe their gods are sinful.

Six of ten people in Calcutta live on the street. There are 660 million people in India, and fifteen million die every year. Twenty-seven million are born, so they just keep getting more and more people living on the streets. Is it because they don't have any food? No.

Here is one reason: They worship as many as 330 million deities. Everyone has his own. The supreme deity that sits on the top of the pile is the one who goes by one of three names, depending on how it manifests itself: Vishnu, Brahma, or Siva. But under that comes a plethora of gods, personified in the cows.

The cows are supposedly the incarnations of the gods. They then become the centers of worship. Everything that comes from a cow is sacred, including its excretions. To a Hindu, to kill and eat a cow is worse than cannibalism. But get this: cows eat 20 percent of the food supply in India.

They have rest homes for old cows who cease to give milk. Not for old people, just old cows. Every cow eats enough for seven people.

Fifteen percent of the food supply of India is eaten by mice, but nobody kills mice either, because they might be killing a relative. In the Hindu system, one is saved by stopping one's births. They believe a person is born over and over, and Nirvana, or the state of nothingness that one desires, is reached when one no longer gets reborn.

You can be born into the animal kingdom or the people kingdom, and you want to keep getting higher and higher in the caste system. If you drop into the animal kingdom because you've done some bad things while you were a human, there are eighty-four thousand different levels of animal kingdoms you can go through to get out again.

So each animal is somebody on his way up or down. You don't want to kill an animal, because you might be messing up the cycle of karma by pushing someone into another life not intended for him. You might find yourself an animal the next time around. Salvation then comes through an endless cycle of births until one reaches Nirvana.

The social effects of this religious system are beyond description. If you see a poor, wretched, destitute individual with nothing, you do not try to meet his need, because the only way he can get from that level to the next is to do penance where he is. There is no regard for human life. The typical Hindu response to a beggar is *I hope he can work himself out of it.*

What has deprived India is paganism. Without a Christian heritage, without the power of God in a society through the influence of believing people, there is no proper view of man. God feeds his people, and He also feeds those who are not His people when they hang around with His people. Apart from belonging to Him, there is no guarantee. There isn't ever going to be enough for the world of people who don't know God, because God is the source.

Matthew 6:25 indicates that God does not want us to preoccupy ourselves with the physical. He is saying that He will take care of that. "Therefore I say unto you, Take no thought for your life, what ye shall eat, or what ye shall drink; nor yet for your body, what ye shall put on." He takes care of the birds (v. 26), the lilies (vv. 28-29), and the grass (v. 30). Then why are you (v. 31) worrying about what we'll eat? What we'll drink? Or what we'll be clothed with? Verse 32, "For after all these things do the Gentiles seek: for your heavenly Father knoweth you have need of these things."

Verse 33 tells us to seek first the kingdom of God and His righteousness, "and all these things shall be added unto you." God is saying, "I will take over this area if you'll just acknowledge that I'm the source of it. You don't have to get stuck at that level, and you can invest your life in the kingdom."

He supplies our need in two ways. First, (Genesis 3:19) man is to earn his bread by the sweat of his face.

We are not supposed to say, "Oh, I'm busy being spiritual so I'm waiting for the ravens to bring me food," or, "Could you grow me a gourd, Lord? It's warm out here." No. We are to work.

First Timothy 5:8 says, "But if any provide not for his own, he is worse than an infidel."

Paul really hits the nail on the head in 2 Thessalonians 3:10: "For even when we were with you, this we commanded you, that if any would not work, neither should he eat."

There are some, of course, who cannot work, and we also have to meet their needs. Although Paul's heart went out to those in need to the point where he would scour Asia Minor collecting money to take back to the poor saints of Jerusalem, at the same time he had no sympathy for someone who was poor simply because he would not work.

God supplies our needs through our own efforts, and through the generosity and the graciousness of others around us.

What about Hebrews 11, where the saints of God, of whom the world was not worthy, were persecuted, went without places to sleep, had no food, and were destitute, forsaken, naked, and some even martyred? Doesn't that contradict what we have just said? No.

God supplies our needs until it is time for us to die, that's all. He may choose to take us home to be with Him through a lack of the sufficiencies. But until that time in his sovereign plan, our needs will be met. And when the physical life ends, we enter into an inconceivable abundance.

When we pray, "Give us this day our daily bread," we are saying that we trust God as the source to supply all the physical needs of our lives, and we affirm that because we are His children walking in righteousness, obedience, and in willing submission to His will, we know He will take care of all those things. We lift our hearts in gratitude while setting our affections on things above.

Our *substance* is bread.

The *source* is God.

Our *supplication* is "give."

Who are the *seekers*? We are. The church of Christ is not isolated. "Give us" embodies all the Christian community.

The *schedule*? "This day." In its simplicity it says, "One day at a time, Father, I accept Your provision." It stresses the contentment we have when we live with a day-by-day confidence in God and do not worry about the future.

9

"And Forgive Us Our Debts"—The Pardon of Prayer, Part 1

The most essential and the most blessed and the most costly thing God ever did was to provide man the forgiveness of sin.

It is most essential because it keeps us from hell and gives us joy in this life.

It is most blessed because it introduces us into a fellowship with God that goes on forever.

And it is most costly because it cost the Son of God His life.

Forgiveness of sin is the greatest need of the human heart, because sin has a twofold effect. It promises to damn men forever while at the same time robbing them of the fullness of life by burdening the conscience with unrelenting guilt.

Sin is unquestionably the major problem in the life of man.

Psychiatrist William Sadler says, "A clear conscience is a great step toward barricading the mind against neuroticism."

John R. W. Stott, in his little book *Confess Your Sins*, quotes the head of a large British hospital: "I could dismiss half my patients tomorrow if they could be assured of forgiveness."

Forgiveness is man's deepest need now and in the future, for health and for heaven. Thus it is the first petition related to man's soul in the Disciples' Prayer. This is where God and man must meet. For before God can ever lead us at all (let alone lead us not into temptation), before He can deliver us from anything, we must have a relationship to Him that is possible only when our sins are dealt with.

He is a holy God of purer eyes than to behold evil. He cannot look upon iniquity (see Habakkuk 1:13). "Holy, holy, holy is the LORD of Hosts," says Isaiah. There is no way that holy God can possibly entertain a relationship with unholy men unless there is forgiveness of sin.

Let's consider four principles in this phrase, which we will cover in this and the next two chapters:

Principle one—Sin makes man guilty and brings judgment. That is really the focal point of the human dilemma. Man is a sinner, and that is his problem. The Bible says sin is disobedience, lawlessness, breaking God's law, violating His standard. Romans 3:19 says we are therefore "guilty before God."

Romans 6:23 says that because we are guilty, the wages of our sin, the penalty, the sentence, is death. So in breaking God's laws, man becomes guilty and faces death.

Principle two—Forgiveness is offered by God on the ground of Christ's death. The holy God who sees a sinful society is also a merciful, loving, and forgiving God who sees man's need. Though man is guilty and stands in judgment, God is a forgiving God. The Bible says He will remember our sin no more; He will pass by our iniquities; He will bury them in the depths of the sea; He will remove them as far as the east is from the west.

Throughout the prophets and the apostles of the Scriptures there is this unceasing promise: He wants to forgive our sins. But in His holiness, He could not do that. He had to bear the penalty for our sins. The Bible tells us that Christ bore in His own body the sins of all the people who ever lived, and paid the price of death for every man. He is the propitiation, or the covering, for the sins of the whole world. He became sin for us, He who knew no sin. A just and righteous and holy God cannot forgive sin unless the penalty is paid. So Christ took our place.

Principle three—Confession of sin is necessary to receive that forgiveness from God. Paul says in Acts 20:21, "Repentance toward God and faith toward our Lord Jesus Christ" results in salvation.

First John 1:9 says, in effect, that the ones confessing their sins are the ones giving evidence that they are being forgiven. No man receives salvation who is not repentant for sin.

God is eager to forgive the one who confesses.

Principle four, the knockout punch of this passage—Forgiving one another is an essential part of receiving forgiveness for ourselves. Don't be confused, although it looks like forgiveness from God requires that we forgive somebody else. It's not that you have to start forgiving people before you can get saved. You *can't* really forgive somebody else if you are not a Christian. How can you do a righteous act before you have a righteous nature? That raises a basic misunderstanding of verses 14 and 15 following the Disciples' Prayer, which we will discuss in the next chapter.

Now let's take four words from those four principles and deal with them individually.

Sin makes us guilty.

Forgiveness is offered by God.

Confession is necessary.

And *forgiving* one another is essential.

Those four words, fully understood, can literally open the meaning of this often confusing portion of Scripture.

Sin. Romans 3:10 says, "As it is written, there is none righteous, no, not one." The Lord added that last part because it is certain that if He had simply said, "There is none righteous," somebody would have said, "Comma, except me." So the Lord says there is none righteous, no, not even you.

Verse 12 says they have all "gone out of the way," that is, they have all departed from the way of righteousness. "They are together become unprofitable" (the Greek word means to go sour like bad milk).

Verse 19 says, "Now we know that what things soever the law saith, it saith to them who are under the law: that every mouth may be stopped." In other words, there's no defense. You have nothing to say to justify yourself, "and all the world may become guilty before God."

Verse 23: "For all have sinned, and come short of the glory of God."

Romans 5 goes on to say that in Adam all have died and sin has passed upon them all. Sin stirs up cosmic chaos. Sin attacks every baby born into the world. In Psalm 51:5, David said, "In sin did my mother conceive me."

Sin is the monarch of the world that rules the heart of every man. Sin is the first lord of the soul. Sin's virus has contaminated every living being.

Sin is the degenerative power in the human stream that makes man susceptible to disease, illness, death, and hell.

Sin is the culprit in every broken marriage, every disrupted home, every shattered friendship, every argument, every pain, every sorrow, every anguish, and every death.

Sin is the common denominator.

No wonder Scripture says in Joshua 7:13 that sin is that "accursed thing." It is compared to the venom of a snake. It is compared to the stench of death. And tragically, from the viewpoint of human resources, absolutely nothing can be done about it.

Jeremiah said, "Can the Ethiopian change his skin or the leopard his spots? then may ye also do good, that are accustomed to do evil" (13:23). It's hopeless.

Sin dominates the mind. Romans 1:21 indicates that men have a reprobate mind, a mind given over to evil and lust.

Sin dominates the will. According to Jeremiah 44, men will to do evil because their will is controlled by sin.

Sin dominates the emotions and the affections, according to John 3:19: "Men loved darkness rather than light."

Sin brings men under the control of Satan. Ephesians 2:2 teaches that men are guided by "the prince of the power of the air, the spirit that now worketh in the children of disobedience."

Sin brings people under divine wrath, says Ephesians 2:3.

Sin makes life utterly miserable, Job says in chapter 5, verse 7: "Man is born unto trouble, as the sparks fly upward."

Isaiah 48:22; "There is no peace, saith the LORD, unto the wicked."

Romans 8:20 says, "The creature was made subject to vanity [emptiness]."

So man's whole life is stained with sin. And the 50 million or so that die every year face the ultimate consequence of it.

The Bible takes great care to present to man the full meaning of sin. There are five New Testament words for sin. First, *hamartia*, Greek for "missing the mark." It is used 137 times in the text and is an archer's word. Generally, the idea is that you miss because your arrow falls short. Some people's arrows go farther than others, but nobody's gets there.

We miss the mark. What is the mark? In Matthew 5:48, our Lord said, "Be ye . . . perfect, even as your Father which is in heaven is perfect." When we are like God we hit the mark, and when we aren't, we don't. Welcome to the community of those who miss the mark.

The second New Testament word for sin is *parabasis*. It means to step across a line, God's line between right and wrong. It is doing what is forbidden in thought, in word, or in act.

Third, the word *anomia*, based on the word *nomos* (or law) means lawlessness. This is a flagrant rebellion against God.

Notice the progression in these words. *Hamartia* speaks more of our basic incapacity, our nature. *Parabasis* means we just can't restrain ourselves from the forbidden area, a little more flagrant than *hamartia*. *Parabasis* is more self-directed, more premeditated.

But when you come to *anomia*, that is open, flagrant rebellion. This describes the man who does not want God making any claim on his life.

Then we come to the fourth and fifth words, the words used in the phrase in question and in Matthew 6:14-15 following the Disciples' Prayer. The fourth word is trespass, or *paraptoma*, which means to slip or fall (see Galatians 6:1).

Fifth, debt, or *opheilema*, is a very interesting word. It is used only here in Romans 4 as a noun, but its verb form is used many times. It is a word not that familiar to us in terms of sin. But the verb form is used thirty times, twenty-five in a moral sense, and it means to owe a debt. When you sin, you owe to God a consequence.

At the end of the age, at the great white throne judgment, God will judge the ungodly out of the books (Revelation 20:11-15). What books? The books that record the unpaid debts.

Among the rabbis and the Jews of Matthew's day, the most common word for debt was *hova*, an Aramaic word also meaning responsibility. When you read about the Disciple's Prayer in Luke, Luke says, "Forgive us our trespasses" because he speaks in possibly a more classical manner. But Matthew, with his Jewish orientation, zeroes in on his concept of debt because he knows his Jewish audience.

We owe such a massive debt to God because of our unrelenting sin that we could never pay it off. Even Peter said, "Depart from me; for I am a sinful man, O Lord" (Luke 5:8).

Even Paul said he was the chief of sinners (1 Timothy 1:15).

Jesus taught all men everywhere to pray, "Forgive us our debts," and in so doing He laid out the universality of the problem of sin. The Holy Spirit came into the world, says John 16, to convict of sin.

Any man who honestly faces the reality of his character cannot be other than conscious of his debt to God and his need to be forgiven.

Forgiveness. If sin is the problem, forgiveness is the provision. Forgiveness is God's passing by our sin. It is His wiping our sin off the record. It is God's setting us free from punishment and guilt.

It is essentially bound up in what Micah 7:18-19 says: "Who is a God like unto thee, that pardoneth iniquity and passeth by the transgression of the remnant of His heritage? He retaineth not His anger for ever, because He delighteth in mercy. He will turn again, He will have compassion upon us; He will subdue our iniquities; and thou wilt cast all their sins into the depths of the sea."

Isn't that great? God in the Old Testament says "I will remember their sin no more" (Jeremiah 31:34). It can be summed up in four simple statements: Forgiveness is taking away our sin, covering our sin, blotting out our sin, and forgetting our sin.

Isaiah 53:6 says He has taken the iniquity of us all and laid it on Christ.

Psalm 85:2 says, "Thou hast covered all their sin."

Isaiah 43:25 says, "I am he that blotteth out thy transgressions."

And He remembers our sins no more. God literally eliminates our sin.

If we ever get to the place in our Christian lives where this becomes commonplace, we have lost that joy of understanding forgiveness and have hit a dry place. How thankful we should be for such a forgiveness! It is only possible because of Christ.

God could not pass by our sin unless He placed the punishment for it on someone else, and that is why Christ Jesus died.

There are two kinds of forgiveness. One is judicial forgiveness, and the other let's call "relational" forgiveness.

Judicial forgiveness views God as a judge. He says, "You're guilty, you've broken the law, you're under judgment, condemnation. There has to be punishment."

But then that same Judge says, "On the basis of Christ's death, He bore your punishment. He took your guilt. He paid for your sin. The price is accomplished. I declare you forgiven."

Through salvation, full, complete, positional forgiveness is granted by God as the moral judge of the universe. And by that act of judicial forgiveness, all our sins—past, present, future, committed, being committed, and to be committed—are totally, completely, and forever forgiven, and we are justified from all things forever.

When does that happen? The moment you invite Jesus Christ into your life. The moment you are redeemed. The moment you place your faith in Christ, your sin is put on Him and His righteousness is put on you, and God judicially declares you justified.

Declared righteous—positionally and forever, all sin covered, passed over, blotted out, and forgiven. Oh, what a thought!

And it is all because of what Christ did on the cross. In Matthew 26:28 He said as He held the cup, "This is my blood of the new testament, which is shed for many for the remission of sins."

In Ephesians 1:7 Paul said, "In whom [Christ] we have redemption through his blood, the forgiveness of sins."

In 1 John 2:12, "I write unto you, little children, because your sins are forgiven you for his name's sake."

Ephesians 4:32, "Even as God for Christ's sake hath forgiven you."

Colossians 2:13, "And you, being dead in your sins and the uncircumcision of your flesh, hath he quickened together with him, having forgiven you all trespasses; blotting out the handwriting of ordinances that was against us . . . and took it out of the way, nailing it to his cross."

In those days a criminal was crucified with the record of his crimes nailed at the top of the cross for all the world to see why he was being executed. The apostle Paul was saying that when Jesus died on the cross, God pulled all the pages out of the sin books, stacked them all together, nailed them to the cross as if they were the crimes of Jesus, and when Jesus died He paid the penalty, and God blotted them out.

That is judicial forgiveness. Oh, to know that we are ultimately and forever forgiven in Christ is tremendous joy! We can say with Paul in Romans 8:34, "Who is he that condemneth?" If God, the highest Judge in the universe, declares me just, who's going to condemn me? Therefore, nothing shall separate me from the love of Christ.

We'll discuss relational forgiveness in the next chapter, but before we do let's look now at Hebrews 10, where the writer is comparing the sacrificial system of Israel with the sacrifice of Christ. In verse 10 he says, "We are sanctified by the offering of the body of Jesus Christ once for all."

Sanctified means to be made pure, made holy, set apart, separated. We are made holy by the one sacrifice of Christ. When He died and we believed, his sacrifice was sufficient. He said on the cross, "It is finished."

In contrast to that, in verse 11, the priests in the

Old Testament were daily ministering, and they were offering the same sacrifices again and again, always standing because the job was never done. Verse 12, "But this man [Christ], after he had offered one sacrifice for sins for ever, sat down." Why? It was over!

Verse 14, "For by one offering He hath perfected for ever them that are sanctified."

Jesus says in Matthew 5:48, "Be ye perfect," and then goes to the cross and perfects us. Christ is the solution to the sin problem.

10

"And Forgive Us Our Debts"—The Pardon of Prayer, Part 2

Sin, though forgiven, is a reality in a Christian's life. When you got saved you did not all of a sudden stop sinning. There should be a decreasing frequency of sin, along with an increasing sensitivity to it, but a Christian who says he does not sin is in a desperate situation. If he really thinks he's not sinning, neither is he seeking the solution.

There are some who teach that Christians reach certain levels in their lives when they don't sin anymore. That isn't true. We continue to sin. That's why we need more than just judicial forgiveness. We need relational forgiveness. One deals with eternal position, the other with daily practice.

Now we are dealing with God not as a righteous Judge but as a loving Father. Even though we have been judicially forgiven and that is settled eternally, we still sin, don't we? And when we sin, something happens in our relationship to God. The relationship does not end, but something is lost in the intimacy of it.

Let me illustrate from Psalm 51. Righteousness had been imputed to David's account. He believed God. He loved God. He trusted God. His faith was in God. He had received redemption. But he fell into sin, terrible sin—adultery and then murder.

Notice the nature of his prayer in this psalm, because this is the prayer that came out of his guilt-ridden, blood-stained heart as he reflected on his sin. Verse 11, "Cast me not away from Thy presence; and take not Thy Holy Spirit from me."

David was speaking about something that he did not want to happen, not something that had happened. God's presence was still with David, and so was God's Holy Spirit.

David was saying, "Don't let it go further than it has. Don't take that away." And for us God never will.

Look at verse 14. "Deliver me from blood guiltiness, O God, thou God of my salvation." David affirmed that God was still the God of his salvation. He cried to a God whose presence was there, whose Spirit was there, whose salvation he possessed yet.

But even in affirming that the judicial forgiveness was there, David could not help but feel the loss of something intimate in the relationship. And that's what he meant when he cried out in verse 2, "Wash me throughly from mine iniquity, and cleanse me from my sin. For I acknowledge my transgressions: and my sin is ever before me. Against thee, thee only, have I sinned, and done this evil in thy sight."

Verse 7, "Purge me with hyssop, and I shall be clean: wash me, and I shall be whiter than snow."

Verse 8, "Make me to hear joy and gladness; that the bones which thou hast broken may rejoice." He wanted the joy back.

Verses 10-12, "Create in me a clean heart, O God; and renew a right spirit within me. . . . Restore unto me the joy of thy salvation."

He didn't say, "Restore thy salvation;" he said, "Restore unto me the *joy* of it."

I can be forgiven, but if I am sinful and unconfessing and unrepentant in that sinfulness, I forfeit the joy of the fullness of that relationship.

In 1 John 1:3, John wrote, "That which we have seen and heard declare we unto you, that ye also may have fellowship with us: and truly our fellowship is with the Father, and with His Son Jesus Christ." He preached Christ because of judicial forgiveness. Then he went a step further.

Verse 4 says, We write in order "that your joy may be full." He's saying on the one hand, "We preach the gospel so that you'll come into the fellowship," and on the other hand, "We write the epistle so that in the fellowship you will know the fullness of joy." His first prerequisite for joy is that you keep confessing your sins (v. 9).

In John 13, our Lord spoke of His love for the disciples, in spite of their waywardness and sinfulness, in spite of the fact that they were sitting around arguing who would be given the chief honors in the kingdom. They were self-centered, selfish, possessive, indifferent to Christ, unconcerned about His impending death, arguing, proud, egotistical, very ugly.

In the midst of it all, the dear Lord took off His outer garment and put a towel around His waist and started to wash their feet. Humiliating to Him and to them. *They* should have done it for *Him*.

He came to Peter (v. 8), and Peter said, "You'll never wash *my* feet." I believe Peter was facing his own sin. He had been arguing about who was to be the greatest in the kingdom and was the epitome of the insensitivities listed above.

Jesus answered him, "If I wash thee not, thou hast no part with me."

He was saying, in effect, "Peter, if you want to really know what it is to fellowship with Me, if you want to know what it is to be part of what I am, if you want the fullness of Our relationship, you'd better let Me wash your feet."

Then Peter said, "Lord, don't wash my feet only—wash my hands and my head."

Jesus replied, "He that is washed needeth not save to wash his feet."

In other words, "Peter, I want to wash only your feet."

There is a tremendous spiritual truth here. Christ was saying, "You are already clean. You've already been redeemed. You've already been made righteous by faith. I'm not talking about bathing you all over again. I'm interested in keeping the dirt off your feet."

They had already had their spiritual baths when they believed. They had judicial forgiveness. All that was necessary now was for Christ to keep the fullness of their relationship open by washing their feet—relational forgiveness.

Once you have been cleaned, bathed in the saving blood of Jesus Christ, you've received judicial forgiveness that does not have to be extended again. But relational forgiveness goes on every day as we keep the fullness of the communion open. Positional purging needs no repetition, but practical purging must be repeated daily.

Somewhere in our prayers, after we have acknowledged His name be hallowed and His kingdom come and His will be done, and after we have acknowledged that God is the source of our physical and daily sustenance, we need to face the fact that our feet are dirty. And we need to acknowledge the fact that as long as they're dirty and we're unconfessing and unrepenting, there is a loss in the fullness of joy in the intimacy, the communion, that we can have with God.

Think again of David. Nathan had told him, "The Lord has put away your sin."

But not long afterward David wrote in Psalm 32:5, "I acknowledged my sin unto thee, and mine iniquity have I not hid. . . . I will confess my transgressions unto the LORD."

He already knew that the judicial element was cared for, yet still he cried out in confession to open the parental channel and keep the intimacy of the relationship.

So the message of this petition, "Forgive us our debts" is simply a plea that we experience the moment-by-moment cleansing that comes when we acknowledge our sin to the Lord. Very basic. Very necessary.

What thrills me is God's eagerness to forgive. If you were in some pagan religion, you might believe God to be like men—that He gets so sick of hearing you that one day He just says, "This is the last time. From here on out, you take the consequences. I've given you more forgiveness than any ten people deserve."

But the Old Testament says, "Thou art a God ready to pardon" (Nehemiah 9:17).

Micah 7:18 says, "He delighteth in mercy." Mercy is an act of His nature that gives Him glory, for we glorify a merciful God.

That is why Romans 5:20 says, "Where sin abounded grace did much more abound." God loves

to forgive. And you know you can take all the forgiveness He has and it won't diminish His resources at all. You can come back as many times as
you want, and it will never diminish His love.
Never.

Because our sin is covered for eternity, shall we
just go out and commit sin? Hardly. If I know God
has forgiven all my sins and that no matter how
many times I come back and ask His forgiveness
He's eager to give it, that should keep me from
sinning, rather than free me to continue. I can't
abuse that. If anything could ever keep a man
straight, that kind of forgiving love in advance
should do it.

We've seen the *problem:* sin.

We've seen the *provision:* forgiveness.

Let's talk about the *plea:* confession.

The whole of this petition implies confession.
You could know about sin and know about forgiveness, but if you did not confess your sin, you would
never know that joy and rich intimacy with God.
As long as I harbor my sin and never turn from it, I
am never free to know the joy He wants me to
know. A barrier is there that blocks the intimacy of
fellowship. And so I must confess. I must open my
heart and admit my sin. And that is tough, isn't it?

As a little boy I vandalized a school in Indiana
with another child. My father was holding revival
meetings in that small town. The school officials
went from house to house, and when they came to
where we were staying, my father went to the door.

I held my father's hand and applied my most
angelic face to show that I was as spiritual as my
dad and would never be caught doing something
like that. He patted me on the head. "Not Johnny.
Why, he's a wonderful boy."

My father was expressing such love for me, and such confidence, that I was very distraught. That night at the meeting I went forward and told him, "I think I need Jesus in my heart."

He did not know why until ten years later when I finally had the courage to tell him. It's tough to confess. And as long as you don't, you forfeit true intimacy. Proverbs 28:13 says, "He that covereth his sin shall not prosper." Your spiritual prosperity is at stake.

That's why He recommends, and we had better pray, "Forgive us our debts."

I have seen Christians, judically forgiven and eternally secure, who for a time can be so hardened by willful sin, so impentient, so unconfessing, so insensitive to that sin, and so totally joyless that they did not even know the meaning of a loving, intimate fellowship with God. They blocked it out with the barricade of their unconfessed sin. I pray that will not be the case with you or me. Sooner or later, if we are really children of the light, confession will break forth. It is characteristic of a true believer (1 John 1:9).

11

"And Forgive Us Our Debts"—The Pardon of Prayer, Part 3

"For if ye forgive men their trespasses, your heavenly Father will also forgive you: But if ye forgive not men their trespasses, neither will your Father forgive your trespasses" (Matthew 6:14-15). This important comment comes after the prayer. Remember, we are speaking of relational forgiveness—sanctification—not the judicial, positional forgiveness of salvation.

Have you freed others of the bondage of an offense by openly and full-heartedly forgiving them? There are several reasons to forgive one another.

Number one, because such is the character of saints. Christians are those who forgive. Matthew 5:43 says, "Love your enemies, bless them that curse you, do good to them that hate you, and pray for them which despitefully use you, and persecute you; that you may be [manifest that you are] the children of your Father."

When we fail to forgive someone, we set ourselves up as a higher judge than God. God infinitely forgives. As His children, we are to be like Him.

Second, we are to forgive one another because it follows the example of Christ. First John 2:6 says that if we abide in Him we ought to walk as He walked. How did He walk? In forgiveness. Ephesians 4:32 says we are to forgive "one another even as God for Christ's sake" has forgiven us.

Of the very ones who had driven the nails through his hands, of the very ones who had spit upon Him and mocked Him and crushed a crown of thorns upon His blessed head, He said, "Father, forgive them."

None of us has endured what Christ has endured, yet He forgave us all and thus set the pattern.

Third, we are to forgive one another because it expresses the highest virtue of man. Men most manifest the majesty of their creation in the image of God when they express forgiveness. Proverbs 19:11 says, "The discretion of a man deferreth his anger; and it is his glory to pass over a transgression."

An unforgiving heart is an advantage for Satan, according to 2 Corinthians 2, a root of bitterness that binds the conscience (Hebrews 12:15). People who carry bitterness and grudges are literally wounding themselves.

Fourth, we should forgive one another because it delivers us from chastening. An unforgiving spirit is sin. And where there is sin there is chastening. Every disobedient son, whom the Lord loves, He chastens (Hebrews 12:5-11).

First Corinthians 11 points out that animosity toward one another and bitterness and factions turned a love feast into something horrible and vile. Because of that, many of them were weak and sick and some were even dead. The Lord chastened them for a lack of proper love to one another.

But more important than those four reasons, we are to forgive one another because if we don't, we do not receive forgiveness. That is shocking, and many people do not understand Matthew 6:14-15. But this is the *prerequisite*.

The *problem* is sin.

The *provision* is forgiveness.

The *plea* is for confession.

And now we have the *prerequisite:* forgiving others.

The idea is that before we ever seek forgiveness for our own *opheilema* (sin against God), for which we are indebted, we forgive those who have sinned against us. That's pretty potent stuff. Our relationship with the Lord cannot be right until our relationship with others is made right. Jesus clearly referred to this in Matthew 5:23-24: "Therefore if thou bring thy gift to the altar, and there rememberest that thy brother hath ought against thee; leave there thy gift before the altar, and go thy way; first be reconciled to thy brother, and then come and offer thy gift."

Before we come to get our feet washed each day, before we bring our sins and say, "Lord, cleanse me again and use me," we've got to be sure we've forgiven others.

Do you go to church all the time, read your Bible and other Christian books, go to seminars and Bible classes and all the rest and still not have the joy you ought to have? Do you miss out on being used by God and feel your life is not all it could be? Do you get tired of trying to reach a certain spiritual standard?

Maybe the answer is simple. Maybe you're not confessing your sins. You're not going to the Lord and saying, "I am a sinner, I acknowledge it. I admit it. And here are the sins. Purify me."

Maybe you do that and you still don't have the joy. Perhaps you haven't backed up far enough. Perhaps the Lord isn't giving you the release and joy you seek because you still have something cooking with somebody you haven't forgiven. If so, you have short-circuited your own spiritual welfare.

Jesus said, "Give and it shall be given unto you." In whatever measure you mete it out, that's exactly how God will mete it out to you (Luke 6:38). Even the Jews knew that. In 200 B.C. they said, "Forgiveness of your neighbor's wrongdoing means that when you pray your sins will be forgiven too."

The Talmud, the rabbinical commentary on the Old Testament, says, "He who is indulgent toward others' faults will be mercifully dealt with by the supreme Judge himself."

What about your life? Are you forgiving? If you are not, God is not going to forgive you in the relational sense. You will go through life with muddy feet. Judicially you are justified, and the righteousness of Christ is imputed to you, but the joy is gone and the intimacy is gone, and the usefulness is gone.

How do you take care of a grudge? Here are three practical steps.

First, take it to God as a sin. Be willing to repent of it and forsake it.

Second, go to the person. Tough? I'm only telling you this so you can know spiritual joy. Say, "I want to offer my forgiveness to you or seek your forgivness."

Third, give the person something you value very highly. Jesus said, "Where your treasure is, there will your heart be also" (Matthew 6:21). Put something precious to you in his hands, and your heart will go with it and will change the way you feel about him.

There have been times when I've felt something about someone that I shouldn't have felt: bitterness, bad feelings, that I'd been wronged, something like that. I have freed myself of the bondage through this process. When I gave the gift, I really began to express the liberty in my spirit. There is no joy like the joy of giving. That's what the Lord is saying to us here.

No wonder so much of Christianity is short-circuited in its power. There are too many unresolved conflicts with people. If you regard iniquity in your heart, Psalm 66 says, "The Lord will not hear" you.

James 2:13 says, "For he shall have judgment without mercy, that hath shewed no mercy." Don't put yourself in a chastening positon.

Matthew 18 provides us a final illustration to this important truth. The text down to verse 15 deals with the same issue, but in verse 21 Peter says, "Lord, how oft shall my brother sin against me, and I forgive him? till seven times?"

Jesus said, "I say not unto thee, Until seven times: but, Until seventy times seven." Indefinitely, infinitely, unendingly.

Then he begins a story in verse 23. "Therefore is the kingdom of heaven likened unto a certain king, which would take account of his servants. And when he has begun to reckon, one was brought unto him, which owed him ten thousand talents." Now let's stop there a minute.

That servant was a real rat. The worst. Ten thousand talents is so much money that it's hard for us to even conceive. For example, one talent could be worth about six thousand days' work. So it would take this man nineteen years working six days a week to earn *one* talent, and he owed *ten thousand*.

How could a servant ever owe that much? Perhaps he had been pilfering from the king's treasury and had lost it all on a bad investment. He had nothing with which to pay.

If it is inconceivable how he gained that much, imagine what he must have done to lose it all! It's one thing to steal—that's crooked—but it is stupid to lose it all.

The servant therefore fell down and worshiped the king, saying, "Lord, have patience with me, and I will pay thee all."

Now that is *really* stupid. He would have to live 190 years and put every dime he ever earned into his debt. The man was a fool no matter how you look at it. Our reaction might be fury. If we had somebody holding out a couple of thousand dollars on us, we might be basket cases.

But the Lord of this servant was moved with compassion, loosed him, and forgave him the debt. Amazing.

Guess who that king represents? God.

Guess who the servant is? All of us. We owed a debt we could not pay. And He forgave. Why? He was compassionate. How could He forgive a debt as astronomical as that? Because of His great love.

The same servant, in verse 28, went out and found one of his fellow servants who owed him money worth about three months' work. Peanuts. The one who had been forgiven the ten thousand grabbed the other by the neck, the Bible says, and demanded, "Pay me what you owe me."

And the fellow servant fell at his feet and besought him, "Have patience with me, and I will pay thee all." But the evil man cast him into prison.

When the other servants saw what had happened, they told the king, who called the evil one to him. "O you wicked servant," he said. "I forgave you all that debt because you besought me; should not you also have had compassion on your fellow servant even as I had pity on you?" His angry lord delivered him to the inquisitors.

So likewise shall God do unto us if we do not from our hearts forgive everyone who has trespassed against us. That is a picture of somebody who wants to take all the forgiveness God can give but is not willing to give it to somebody else.

That parable has primary application for one who is not truly saved. His redemption has been purchased by God, the gift of forgiveness offered, but his unforgiving, merciless spirit reveals that he has never been redeemed. Thus he is sentenced to pay his own debt—eternally.

But the disciples were also in the audience when Jesus taught, and I can see the scope of this principle broaden to encompass indirectly and secondarily a believer who is unforgiving and merciless, and thus subject to chastening.

Lord Herbert put it very well when he said, "He who cannot forgive others breaks the bridge over which he himself must pass."

12

"And Lead Us Not into Temptation"— The Protection of Prayer

We have been learning to pray. Our teacher has been the Lord Jesus Christ, who has given us this model.

My own praying has been reshaped to fit this pattern, for this Lord's Prayer, Disciples' Prayer, is a skeleton for all praying. The ingredients for this prayer touch every area of need and every element of glorifying and praising God.

It is a prayer that in every phrase and every petition focuses on God, His person, His attributes, and His wonderful works. True prayer is expressing absolute dependence on God. And that is what our Lord is after.

The basic reality of this prayer is the truth about God. Every petition promises something that He already guarantees. God's name will be hallowed. God's kingdom will come. His will is to be done. He has already promised to give us our daily bread, He has already granted us total forgiveness in Christ. And He's already promised that He will lead us away from evil in the path of righteousness.

The more we understand about the promises of
God, the richer our prayers become. The premium
has been paid by Christ, the policy is ours. The
benefits are rendered in our behalf, and all we have
to do is make the claim.

We've noted that all the features of this prayer
speak of God. "Our Father" speaks of God's
paternity; "hallowed be thy name," of God's priority; "thy kingdom come," His program; "thy will
be done in earth, as it is in heaven," His purpose;
"give us this day our daily bread," His provision;
"forgive us our debts, as we forgive our debtors,"
His pardon; and finally, "lead us not into temptation, but deliver us from evil" speaks of God's protection. It ends with God's preeminence in the
great closing doxology.

The first three petitions relate to God and His
glory. The last three relate to man and his need. We
come then to verse 13, the sixth and final petition:

"Lead us not into temptation, but deliver us from
evil." At first it seems clear, almost simple. It's like,
"Keep us out of trouble, God."

But as we look a little closer, several questions
arise.

Do we have to ask God to not lead us into temptation?

Can a holy, righteous, pure, undefiled, blameless, unblemished, virtuous God possibly lead
anybody into temptation?

And if we do not ask Him to deliver us from evil,
is He going to lead us into evil? The term *temptation*
is neutral. On one hand, it can refer to a solicitation
to evil. In that case God has no part.

James 1:13 says, "Let no man say when he is
tempted, I am tempted of God: for God cannot be
tempted with evil, neither tempteth he any man."

On the other hand, it can refer to a trial or test for our good. If we say, "Don't lead us into a trial, Lord," are we denying another verse in James 1 that says to count it all joy when you enter into a trial? You can see the dilemma, can't you?

I think Chrysostrom, the early church Father, was right when he said that this particular petition is the most natural appeal of human weakness as it faces danger. In other words, it is not so cognitive as it is emotional. It's the cry of the heart that despises and hates the potential of sin.

I realize that trials do a perfecting work and also that God does not tempt me, so I am faced with a paradox not unlike the one in Matthew 5 (rejoice when you're persecuted) and Matthew 10 (flee persecution).

Are we supposed to stand there and rejoice, or run? There is a sense in which we run from persecution, but when it catches us we can know joy in the midst of it. Even our dear Lord said, "Father, let this cup pass from Me" (Mark 14:36). There was something in His humanness that did not want that suffering. Yet He endured the cross for the joy that was set before him (Hebrews 12:2).

I pray this because I know I am a sinner, because I sense my debt and have gone through the pain of confession so many times. I am battered and bruised by a fallen world around me that continues to bump me. So I ask, "God, deliver me from these things." But I accept the fact that such struggles strengthen me.

I don't know about you, but I have to set a watchman over my eyes, another over my ears, another over my tongue. I have to be careful where I go and what I see and whom I talk to (and about what) because I don't trust myself. And when I get

into a trying situation, I rush into the presence of
God like the sentry who doesn't fight the enemy
himself but runs to tell the commander. I retreat to
the presence of God and I say, "I will be over-
whelmed unless You come to my aid."

The kingdom child realizes that he lives in a fall-
en world that pounds against him with temptations
he can never resist in his own humanness.

The natural world is fallen. Men face volcanoes,
earthquakes, fires, floods, pestilence, accidents,
disease, and death.

The intellectual world is fallen. Man's judgments
are partial and unfair. He careens on in the chaos of
relativistic thinking to an inevitable destruction.
Propelled by his own bias, logic is ruled by pride.
Intellects are ruled by lust. Material gain makes
liars out of men. There is a constant colliding of
human opinions.

The emotional world is fallen. Grief and care and
anxiety rule. The inability to handle attitudes
shrivels man's spirit. His soul is chafed by the rub-
bing together of life with life. Envy stings him, hate
embitters him, greed eats away at him.

His affections are misplaced. His love is tram-
pled. His confidence is betrayed. Rich, he steps on
the poor. Poor, he seeks to dethrone the rich. Pris-
ons and hospitals and mental institutions mark the
moral and emotional upheaval of man.

The spiritual world is the darkest and thickest
blackness of all. Man is out of harmony with God.
The machinery is visibly out of gear. He's running
out of "sync" with God's divine plan. Evil tenden-
cies dominate man from his tainted fallen ancestry.
He may want to do right, but he feels pulled down
by some irresistible gravity of evil.

It is a fallen world. It isn't bad enough that the

flesh is fallen, but Satan is also relentlessly attacking. We live in this knowledge, praying, "And lead us not into temptation." We sin because we are tempted internally by our lusts and externally by the enticements of Satan. When lust conceives it brings forth sin. And sin results in death.

How does Satan tempt us? Through the lust of the eyes, the lust of the flesh, and the pride of life. Those do not proceed from the Father. God's desire is that we watch and pray and do not enter into temptation.

The word *temptation* is from the Greek *peirasmos,* which is used over and over in the Scripture. It is simply a test, or a trial. The English word means "seduction to evil," but the Greek word is neutral, sometimes translated "test," sometimes "prove," sometimes "trial," and sometimes "temptation."

In the Disciples' Prayer the word should be translated "trial." So, "Lead us not into trials, or testings."

Any time there is a legitimate trial, or test, there is the possibility of passing or failing. So when God brings a trial, there is always the possibility that the trial can be turned into a temptation.

Joseph said in Genesis 50:20, regarding his brothers' selling him into Egypt, "You meant it for evil, but God mean it for good."

When the prayer says, "Lead us not into trials," I believe the implication is, "Lord, don't lead us into a trial that will present to us a temptation such that we will not be able to resist it."

You walk along and you encounter a certain person or situation, a certain magazine, a certain book, a certain movie theater, a certain program on television—those are all tests. They can show your spiritual strength and cause you to grow, or you can fail and the experiences can turn into temptations that incite your lusts and draw you into sin.

The petition in question is a safeguard against presumption and against a false sense of security. When you think you stand, take heed lest you fall.

The word "into" is *eis* in the Greek, and some have compared it to the Hebrew *liyadh*, which means "into the power of" or "into the hands of." In other words, we are praying, "Do not cause us to be led into the hands of the trial."

Our Lord prayed the same prayer in John 17:15 when He said to the Father, "I pray not that thou shouldest take them out of the world, but that thou shouldest keep them from the evil [one]."

Martin Luther said, "We cannot help being exposed to the assaults, but we pray that we may not fall and perish under them."

When trials come, Satan wants to make us angry and bitter. How do we deal with them? James 4:7 gives us the simple word. "Submit yourselves therefore to God." How do we do that?

We get under His lordship. That means we're going to do what He says. We're going to live in submission to biblical principles. Submitting to God is not some esoteric thing. It is not intellectual suicide or escapism. Submitting to God is ordering one's life to respond in accord with the biblical revelation of God's will.

And so in the midst of trial I say, "O God, I need Your strength infused in me, and I submit to the truths of Your Word. My responses, attitudes, actions, and thoughts are all in submission to Your Word."

It is His Word that prunes the branches in John 15. It is His Word that is hidden in our hearts that we might not sin (Psalm 119). It is His Word that is the sword that defends us against the attack (Ephesians 6).

As we submit to the truths of His Word and take up the sword of God and begin to put it to use in our lives, we resist the devil and he flees. We cry with Christ, "Father, spare me the trial, but if the trial fits Your wisdom and Your way and Your plan, protect me so that I can survive it and grow."

Will God hear this prayer? Yes, based on 1 Corinthians 10:13, one of the greatest verses in the Bible.

"There hath no temptation [*peirasmos*, trial from Satan] taken you but such as is common to man: but God is faithful, who will not suffer you to be tempted [*peirazo*, tried or tested] above that ye are able." Never.

You can never say, "It was too much for me." He will always with the trial provide the way out.

John 18 illustrates that so powerfully. Jesus was in the garden. He had come to be captured by the fort soldiers, who were led by officers of the chief priests and Pharisees. They came with their lanterns and their weapons, and Jesus said to them: "Whom do you seek?"

"Jesus of Nazareth."

He made them say that two times, because that was exactly what He wanted them to utter. They had no right to take anybody but Him. He made them admit that publicly. He answered in John 18:8, "I have told you that I am He. If therefore ye seek me, let these go their way," referring to the eleven disciples with him.

Why did He say that? Verse 9: "That the saying might be fulfilled, which He spake, Of them which Thou gavest me have I lost none." He would not let His disciples enter a trial that they could not endure (1 Corinthians 10:13).

The Lord will hear your prayer because He cares about His own and will lose none, no not one. He will never let you get into a situation that is more than you can handle.

The prayer closes with a doxology: "For Thine is the kingdom, and the power, and the glory, for ever. Amen." You don't dissect it. You just say it, think it, and offer it to God.

There is some evidence that Jesus didn't even say that. That's why it is not included in some of the versions of the Bible. Some manuscripts have it and some do not, but I'll tell you one thing—it's true.

It seems a fitting climax. Some commentators say it would have to have been included originally because the Jews would never have closed a prayer on a negative note. Whether Jesus said it or not, it's an echo of 1 Chronicles 29:11: "Thine, O LORD, is the greatness, and the power, and the glory, and the victory, and the majesty: for all that is in the heaven and in the earth is thine; thine is the kingdom, O LORD, and Thou art exalted as head above all." And with that glorious doxology, we are right back to where we began with the first three petitions in this prayer.

What have we learned from the Disciples' Prayer? That all we need is available to us. God gets His rightful place in the first three petitions, and then our needs are brought to Him and met in His wonderful, eternal supply.

Father, we echo this prayer in our hearts. Deliver us from evil. Deliver us from sin's penalty, dominion, and guilt.

Deliver our wills from bondage, our judgments from perversion, our imaginations from falsehood. Deliver our instincts from sinful drifting.

Deliver our affections from what is earthly. Deliver us from weakness that we may know the fullness of Your strength.

Thank You for this prayer. Your name be hallowed, Your kingdom come, Your will be done.

Continue to give us abundantly our daily bread. Help us to be forgiving others that we may know the fullness of Your forgiveness. And thank You for the promise that You'll never lead us into anything we can't handle.

Help us meet the conditions to know the fulfillment of the inestimable promises of this prayer, and to pray as we ought for Your glory, for Yours *is* the kingdom, and the power, and the glory forever. Amen.